CHORAL DIRECTOR'S COMPLETE HANDBOOK

CHORAL DIRECTOR'S COMPLETE HANDBOOK

Lewis Gordon

Parker Publishing Company, Inc.

West Nyack, New York

Library of Congress Cataloging in Publication Data

Gordon, Lewis,
   Choral director's complete handbook.

    1. Choirs (Music) 2. Conducting, Choral. I. Ti-
tle.
MT88.G78   784.9'6   76-57166
ISBN 0-13-133363-1

Printed in the United States of America

To A.K.

A Word from the Author on the

Practical Value of This Book

This book provides a single, comprehensive source of information for the experienced choral director. It is written for those whose mastery of basic skills and concepts has created a need for an advanced yet practical guide.

Both the conductor's personal development and crucial aspects of the choral program are treated with clarity and perspective. Each chapter has been placed in logical order so that, in following this sequence of guidelines and procedures, you will be shown in a step-by-step way how to improve your present professional standing and effectively channel your efforts to achieve a superior choral program.

This handbook is innovative. Many important ideas and concepts are presented and discussed fully for the first time. For example, have you ever stopped to think how pertinent the subject of body language could be for conductors? Chapter 1 discusses this and also includes methods for developing flexible and expressive conducting.

The psychological and sociological aspects of working with singers is another interesting and useful topic, but it has received little attention until now. This subject is fully discussed in Chapter 2 along with specific ways to motivate your vocal performers.

Recently, taxonomies have been used to classify various types of goals and objectives. Chapter 3 makes use of this important tool to help you assess your present status as a choral director. Methods for developing professional skills and gaining useful knowledge are also presented.

The *Choral Director's Complete Handbook* is truly practical, because it provides proven solutions to problems of immediate concern. By reading Chapter 4 you will know how to build your choral program from the ground up through improved methods of recruitment, auditioning, and planning.

Chapter 5 deals with the actual day-to-day management of your organization. This chapter is full of such essential information as how to test the acoustics of a rehearsal room and organizing for public relations. Of particular interest is a section entitled "Raising Money."

Besides being practical, a book of this scope should address itself to artistic matters. Chapter 6 shows you how to choose interesting repertoire and program with maximum musical impact for the conditions under which you will perform. Creative designing of the printed program is also discussed.

If a handbook is to be called complete, it should include sound information based on responsible research. Chapter 7 gives specific guidelines for performing choral music with stylistic accuracy. These insights are based on scholarly evidence but presented in a straightforward, useful way.

Score analysis has often posed problems for choral directors. Either the topic has received superficial coverage in choral books, or the director has had to take a general course in analysis and then find ways to apply what has been learned to his own situation. Chapter 8 takes a thorough look at choral score preparation and features a performance-oriented approach called "Character Analysis."

This book is also technical in the best sense of the word. Chapter 9 offers highly specific, clinical advice for improving vocal performance. This information is based on acceptable teaching practices and tempered by proven success. Of particular concern is a complete listing of vocal ailments encountered along with suggestions for preventing their occurrence or minimizing their severity.

Chapter 10 emphasizes the need for structure, direction, and guidance in rehearsals. Worksheets for immediate and long-range planning are included. The bulk of the chapter outlines a sure-fire approach for learning and polishing music through three phases of development.

Last, but not least, the *Choral Director's Complete Handbook* is thorough. Chapter 11 discusses those factors necessary to bridge the gap from rehearsal room to concert stage. The coordination of instruments with singers and the preparation of the ensemble for another conductor are highlights in this final chapter.

In short, the *Choral Director's Complete Handbook* is a compendium of the latest ideas and concepts necessary to bring both you and your choral program up to maximum effectiveness. Checklists and charts have been provided for direct access to important topics; examples and illustrations have been included for clarification.

Lewis Gordon

Table of Contents

A Word from the Author on the Practical Value
    of This Book 7

1. Developing Expressive Conducting and Communication
    Skills 15

    The Choral Conductor is a Diversified Communicator (15)
    Basic Conducting—What It Must Accomplish (18)
    Shaping Patterns and Gestures to Convey Music's
        Character (21)
    Expression through Body Language (30)
    The Choral Conductor, the Orchestra, and the Baton (33)

2. Working with People Who Sing: How to Use
    Motivational Techniques 38

    Awareness of the Individual and the Group (38)
    Establishing a Viable Rapport (42)
    Leadership Development (47)
    Group Dynamics—The Key to Success (49)

3. Objectives for Professional Growth 53

    Choral Directing Demands Continual Assessment (53)
    Taxonomy of Choral Skills and Knowledge (54)
    Establishing a Personal Resource Center (57)
    Ways to Accumulate Facts, Insights, and Skills (63)
    Broadening Perspective (64)

4. Establishing a Quality Choral Program: Planning and Promotion **66**

Group Purpose Must Be Defined (66)
Selling the Program and Choosing Members (69)
Planning Events (74)

5. How to Manage Choral Groups Efficiently and Effectively **78**

Choosing Facilities, Equipment, and Wardrobe (78)
Accountability and Maintenance (83)
Raising Money (87)
Officers—Figureheads or Crucial Workers? (90)
Organizing for Public Relations (92)

6. Innovative Concert Programming **95**

Repertoire Selection (95)
Matching Music with the Ensemble (97)
Calculation of Performance Conditions (99)
Program Construction (102)
Designing and Supervising the Printed Program (104)

7. Developing Stylistic Accuracy in Choral Performance **111**

Music to 1600 (113)
The Baroque Era (120)
The Classic Period (124)
Romanticism (126)
Twentieth Century Music (130)

8. How to Prepare the Conductor's Score **135**

Examining and Analyzing the Musical Blueprint (135)
Music's Character Traits (139)
Trouble-Shooting for Potential Problems (142)
Marking the Score (145)

9. Working with the Human Voice **147**

Control of the Singing Process (147)

Dealing with Individual Voices and Their
Characteristics (151)
What to Do about Vocal Hygiene (154)
Exercising the Ensemble (157)

10. Techniques for Conducting Effective Rehearsals 174

Rehearsal Activity Planning (174)
Establishing Operational Procedures (178)
Choral Diction (183)
Preparing Choral Music—Phase I (187)
Preparing Choral Music—Phase II (191)
Preparing Choral Music—Phase III (195)

11. Final Preparations for Performance 197

Completing Ensemble Preparation (197)
Coordination of Musical Elements (199)
Concert Facility Arrangements (202)
Conducting the Dress Rehearsal (204)
Pre-Concert Activities (207)
Minimizing Performance Errors (208)

Index **211**

1

Developing Expressive Conducting and Communication Skills

THE CHORAL DIRECTOR IS A
DIVERSIFIED COMMUNICATOR

The choral director is a highly diversified individual. Besides devoting a musical career to the mastery of choral-vocal techniques, he must achieve practical competence in the areas of human relations, organizational management, and the psychology of learning. Obviously, the director must fulfill several important roles. And, undoubtedly, one of the paramount duties is that of "multidimensional communicator." Four basic modes of communication are continually utilized in this capacity.

- Gesticulation
- Verbalization
- Demonstration
- Written communication

Gesticulation
The choral director, as a *conductor*, guides his ensemble in performance through the use of mutually understandable gestures. This functional sign language must satisfy the following requirements:

- Account for time and place within music
- Prepare performers for musical action

- Coordinate and regulate technical aspects of the performance
- Inspire performers to sing artistically and enthusiastically

The conductor must develop his technical abilities beyond the manipulation of beat patterns. The mastery of conducting requires a subconscious integration of right-hand diagrams within a larger framework of expressive gesticulation.

Verbalization

The competent choral director must learn how to transmit verbal information with consciseness. Through the vehicle of speech, he achieves the following:

- Gives directions for implementation
- Explains and clarifies
- Persuades and convinces
- Corrects and offers solutions

In the interest of maintaining momentum and efficiency during rehearsal, the director should avoid unnecessary conversation. Like oil and water, musical performance and long-winded discussions do not usually mix.

On the other hand, verbal communication with the concert audience *is* sometimes desirable for the following reasons:

- To announce last-minute program changes
- To clarify or augment printed program information
- To provide short, paraphrased translations of works to be performed in a foreign language
- To inform the audience of some unusual or salient feature in a particular work

Care must be taken, however, not to disrupt the mood of the concert with trivial talk. Sentences should be well chosen and geared to the nature of the program and its audience.

The director must cultivate an ability to deliver verbal information to performers and listeners with clarity, coherence, and confidence. Sometimes otherwise good directors give an impression of insecurity or disorganization because they have not developed this skill.

Demonstration

Music is in itself a form of communication. Therefore, the proficient choral director must develop the ability to communicate *through music*. This is accomplished by singing or playing. Basically, demonstration should be employed to achieve the following:

- Correct a musical note or passage
- Clarify a desired singing technique or musical effect
- Provide a model for duplication by the ensemble
- Indicate desired phrasing and melodic direction

The importance of demonstration as a mode of communication should not be overlooked. Sometimes musical meaning can only be clarified through actual performance.

Written Communication

The written or printed word often serves as an "organizational catalyst" if utilized properly. For example, a well-written summer letter informing singers of upcoming events and repertoire can have a buoyant effect on initial attendance and motivation. Obviously, written communication should be limited to special occasions or it will lose its impact. Here are some logical purposes:

- To substitute for verbal communication when it is more convenient than telephoning or holding a meeting
- To "officially confirm" important information such as schedules, concert details, and regulations
- To provide public information in the form of press releases, posters, concert programs, and membership inducements
- To correspond with suppliers, tour and transportation agencies, other choral groups, and outside musicians about matters related to the choral program

The ability to write succinctly is a requirement of the profession. The flair for writing with verve and enthusiasm can have an impact in nurturing and maintaining a dynamic choral organization.

On occasion, I have had the opportunity to talk with former classmates about their progress as choral directors. Inevitably, they stress the importance of diversified communication. Some frequently mentioned subjects including the following:

- The importance of persuasion
- The challenge of corresponding
- Maintaining an open rapport with students
- Knowing the right people

BASIC CONDUCTING—WHAT IT MUST ACCOMPLISH

Rudimentary Skills

Rudimentary skills meet the minimum requirements in a particular field or subject area. In choral music both the singers and the conductor must fulfill certain basic responsibilities if performance is to occur. For the conductor these skills fall into two fundamental areas:

- Conducting patterns
- Cues

Conducting Patterns

Some choral directors contend that there is little need for adhering to fundamental conducting patterns. They argue that these patterns are too mechanistic for choral performance, that they interfere with interpretive gesturing. Fortunately, it is possible for the choral director to "have his cake and eat it too." Simply put, a conducting pattern which has been developed into a habitual response can be modified to accommodate musical expression without losing directional integrity. Furthermore, if singers are to develop into musicians, they will need to know where the beat lies. According to Wilhelm Ehmann, noted German conductor and educator,

> There still is no other device in choral work which offers the possibility of the same security, precision, thoroughness and economy of energy as the mastery of a sound time-beating technique.[1]

---

[1] Wilhelm Ehmann, *Choral Directing*. Translated by George D. Wiebe (Minneapolis: Augsburg Publishing House, 1968), p. 114.

Conducting patterns should be mastered to the extent that they will be technically secure and precise under a variety of "battlefield" conditions. Preoccupation with images of printed conducting diagrams must give way to *habitual* responses which are cued by the music itself. This point brings to mind an interesting observation. Often, when conductors attend the concerts of others, they find themselves so involved as listeners that they unconsciously begin to conduct with their fingers. This *habitual*, physical reaction is called a kinesthetic response. Although this type of involvement can be disturbing to others attending the concert, the practice of matching appropriate conducting patterns to unfamiliar performances on radio and recordings is an excellent method for developing metrical perception and spontaneous pattern responses.

Rudimentary skill in performing conducting patterns must include the following capacities:

- Mastery of unusual as well as basic patterns
- Flexibility to adjust the size of patterns to accommodate tempos, dynamics, and choral group size
- Ability to conduct sub-division (divided beat) and one-beat-to-the-measure (three in one, and so on)
- Control of anacrusic entries and syncopated rhythms
- Ability to define articulation
- Control of pauses and holds

Cues

Cues are special signals given to facilitate various actions by performers. Some cues are built into the right hand conducting pattern.

- Preparatory beats serve as cues for general preparation and breath.
- Downbeats and other strokes serve as cues for attacks and releases.

Right hand cues can be reinforced by turning the body in the direction of pertinent performers. Eye contact and nodding are also useful, particularly when you are cueing more subtle entrances.

Most cues, however, are given with the left hand. Besides freeing the other hand so that it can maintain temporal continuity, the left hand can offer an abundant variety of motions which indicate the exact nature of the desired entry. (See Figure 1-1.)

TYPES OF LEFT-HAND CUES

Gesture	Meaning
Finger in air	Warning of upcoming entry
Fist	Firm entry
Legato beckoning gesture with hand	Gentle entry
Thumb and forefinger moved together and released at moment of entry	Pinpoint entry
Slashing, angular motion with arm	Abrupt entry
Continual circular movement	Consecutive entries *on time*

Figure 1-1

The left hand can also be used effectively to control enunciation of words. Final nasal consonants such as "m" or "n" can be coordinated by joining the thumb with one or more fingers. Initial nasal consonants can be transferred to the following vowel by reversing this process. Final aspirates, such as "t" or "p," should be controlled by a precise cutoff.

You should avoid two common pitfalls when you are developing cueing technique.

1. *Do not point when cueing.* This action can be psychologically antagonistic to the performer. Because of its directness, the unspoken reaction of the musician may very well be, "Don't point at me. I know when to come in."

2. *Do not overcue.* Too many entry signals may confuse the performers and camouflage more important gestures.

SHAPING PATTERNS AND GESTURES
TO CONVEY MUSIC'S CHARACTER

Overcoming the Domination of the Bar Line

The techniques developed for conducting orchestras during the early 18th century have had a profound influence on our present-day choral methods. As composers turned to the metrical system, with its measures and recurring accents, orchestra conductors turned to time beating.

Much of our choral repertoire, however, falls stylistically into periods where such an approach goes against the music's temporal and phrasal construction. For example, vocal ensemble music from 15th and 16th centuries is often based on the *tactus,* a fixed system of *unaccented* beats. And contemporary choral music is sometimes characterized by sweeping phrases which, while notated in multi-metrical measures, should be approached as free-flowing musical sentences.

In cases where metrical construction is emphasized, such as in perpetual motion, martial-like, or strict waltz music, emphasis of the downbeat may be helpful. Generally speaking, however, choral conducting is diametrically opposed to time beating. There are three important reasons for this.

- Abrupt time beating tends to fragment the music.
- "Percussive elbows," usually the result of such beating, are aesthetically incompatible with most choral music.
- Jerky motions may cause throatiness and tightness in singers' voices.

Conducting with Compatibility

Choral conducting, if viewed as an artistic endeavor as well as a skillful technique, must have the flexibility to accommodate the "personality" of each work. Therefore, you should not rely on rigid patterns or "stock gestures" such as "the upbeat twitch." Peter Paul Fuchs eloquently refers to flexible, compatible technique as "harmonious gesturing."[2]

---

[2] *The Psychology of Conducting* by Peter Paul Fuchs. © Copyright 1969 by MCA Music, A Division of MCA, Inc., p. 73.

There are essentially three ways to modify conducting patterns to accommodate musical character.

- By melding
- By modifying the horizontal and vertical elements of the pattern
- By employing passive gestures

Melding

The first step in becoming an expressive conductor is to utilize melded patterns where applicable. This fluid technique is characterized by smooth arm and hand movement through the points of a pattern without the creation of any accent. Melding helps to achieve the following musical results:

- It encourages legato singing.
- It promotes a sense of linear melodic direction.
- It sustains musical arc.

According to Elizabeth Green, "The melded gesture is the very soul of *phrasal conducting*."[3]

The meld is best achieved by treating the points of the conducting pattern as imaginary circles or wheels. By maintaining a smooth, steady motion between and around these points, you ensure a controlled meld. (See Figure 1-2.)

Modifying Horizontal and Vertical Elements of the Pattern

With the exception of one-beat-to-the-measure gestures, conventional patterns are comprised of horizontal and vertical elements called strokes.

- The initial downward stroke represents the primary accent of the measure.
- A horizontal stroke, which moves from the conductor's left to his right *across* an imaginary vertical axis, represents the secondary accent.

---

[3]Elizabeth A. H. Green, *The Modern Conductor* (Englewood Cliffs: Prentice-Hall, Inc., 1965), p. 239.

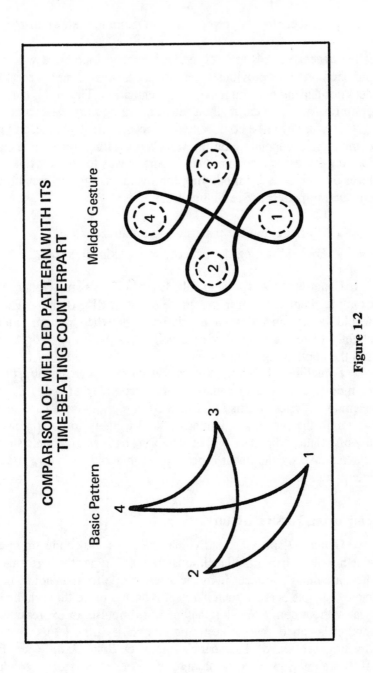

Figure 1-2

- "Filler strokes" represent the remaining beats in the measure.

If the accent strokes are exaggerated, metrical structure will be emphasized. As was previously mentioned, however, most choral music does not depend on such recurrent accentuation. The use of the melded gesture is an excellent method for minimizing metrical accent.

Stress, not to be confused with accent, differs with each musical composition, depending on the work's prevailing dynamic level, performing forces, and texture. One important way to regulate this general level of weight is by modifying the overall height or breadth of the conducting pattern. (See Figure 1-3.)

- By flattening the pattern, you minimize stress.
- By heightening the pattern, you maximize stress.

Usually you will want to enhance the music's stress tendency. For example, Paul Hindemith's delicate chanson "La Biche" (The Doe) would be conducted with a relatively flattened pattern, modified slightly toward a more moderate height for the initial agogic accents and the contrasting forte section.

Sometimes, however, you may want to choose a contrasting type of modified pattern to achieve a more complex effect. J.S. Bach's opening "Kyrie" in his *Mass in B Minor* serves as a case in point. Although the movement is massive and weighty in its approach, the use of a flattened pattern will help to bring out its polyphonic structure. By emphasizing the linear aspect, you can avoid an overly ponderous interpretation.

Employing Passive Gestures

Generally speaking, individual points of the conducting pattern, whether melded or articulated, must have clarity for the performer. But there are many instances in music where *all* performers hold a note for more than one beat. In such places it is best to move through the linked beat without communicating any accent, impulse, or expression. This motion is called passive gesturing. To clarify this, let us look at the opening section of Palestrina's motet *O Bone Jesu*. (See Figure 1-4.) An analysis of each measure of this example from a conducting pattern standpoint reveals the following:

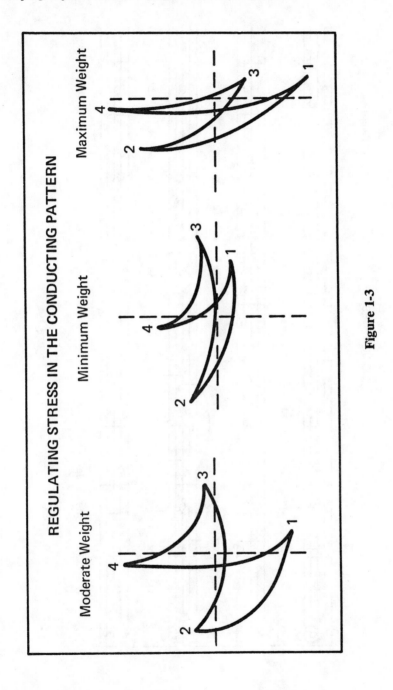

Figure 1-3

Figure 1-4

- Measure 1 should be conducted with an initially *active* downbeat followed by *passive* gesturing throughout the remainder of the pattern.

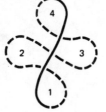

- Measure 2 requires an active downbeat and third beat. Beats 2 and 4 are passive.

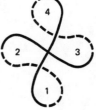

- Measure 3 requires active motion for beats 1, 2, and 4. Beat 3 is passive.

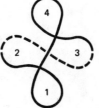

- Measure 4 requires active motion for the first three beats because of the busy tenor line.

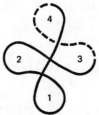

- Measure 5 requires only an incomplete pattern beginning with beat 3 and passively moving through beat 4 because of the held rest.

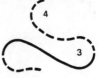

- Measure 6 requires a continuation of passive movement which began on beat 4 of the preceding measure. Only beat 3 is active in this measure.

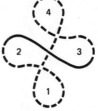

- Measure 7 requires active movement for every beat because of a syncopated tenor line.

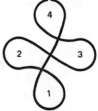

- Measure 8 should be conducted like measure 4.
- Measure 9 requires only a downbeat followed by a delayed release. This final repose should be treated as a chord of indefinite length.

Developing Left Hand Independence

The left hand, although it serves an important function for cueing, should by no means be limited to that role. Although conducting patterns can be modified with the right hand in an effort to approximate the character of the music more closely, the *left hand* is the most important factor in developing expressive conducting.

The development of left hand communication and sense of timing must ultimately be worked out with the ensemble. Through repetition of gestures and verbalization of intention by the choral director, the singers become accustomed to his gestures and intended meaning. The left hand performs two basic expressive functions.

- Shading
- Shaping

1. Shading refers to the control of dynamics, intensity, and articulation. An observation of left hand movements used by various choral conductors reveals several basic shading gestures which appear to convey consistently similar meaning for most singers. (See Figure 1-5.)

LEFT HAND MOVEMENT DYNAMICS

Movement	Psychological Effect	Musical Message
Downward	Quieting	Sing softer
Upward	Climactic	Sing louder
Side-to-side	Smoothing	Maintain same dynamics
Palm out	Restrictive	Controlled intensity
Palm in	Permissive	Project intensity
Angular	Disruptive	Percussive articulation
Circular	Continuity	Legato articulation

Figure 1-5

Singers are not only affected by the *type* of left hand movement but also by its *rate of action*. For example, a slower move creates a relatively conservative response, whereas a sudden, sharp move creates a more lively reaction.

2. Shaping refers to the use of the left hand to lead and control melodic flow. Such gesturing demands complete diversification and

independence of one hand from the other, achieved primarily through practice after patterns have become second nature. Shaping can give melodic line a sense of direction, plasticity, and momentum. Because of the creative nature of shaping, the possibilities of specific gestures are almost limitless. Here are some typical examples:

- Circular movement of the index finger to carry the ensemble through a particular spot
- Slow arc with the entire arm to depict the arsis of a phrase
- High-held hand moved lightly from side to side to suggest a flexible, transparent melodic line

EXPRESSION THROUGH BODY LANGUAGE

Kinesics—The Science of Non-Verbal Communication

Kinesics is a field of study which has exciting implications for the conducting profession. This science is concerned with ways that humans send messages to one another through facial expression, arm and hand movements, and posturing. According to experts in the field, people employ physical behavioral patterns, which are partly learned and partly instinctive, to communicate such basic feelings as hate, fear, joy, and sadness.

Successful choral conductors, perhaps without realizing it, are usually sophisticated body language communicators. Besides achieving technically secure ensemble results through traditional gesturing, they are able to establish contrasting musical moods and elicit a more total effort from singers. Their success results from a capacity to physically show feeling for a musical composition and an ability to communicate their performance demands while conducting.

Avoiding Masking and Shielding

As children grow into adulthood, they begin to build defense mechanisms for protection from society's unwanted intrusions. *Masking* and *shielding* are two basic types of physical defense. The first step in developing skill as a non-verbal communicator is to learn how to avoid these restrictive mechanisms when you are working with choral ensembles.

1.   Masking refers to the practice of immobilizing facial expres-

sion so that emotion or feeling is not conveyed. However, the possibilities in facial communication are too important to overlook. Creating mood for the music at hand through countenance, encouraging singers at points of entry with the eyes, and prolonging alertness and vitality through personal demeanor are just a few examples of utilizing condusive facial expression.

Sometimes conductors unconsciously convey the wrong facial message because of their unawareness of this communicative vehicle. For example, by visually reacting to misinterpreted notes during a performance, the choral leader runs the risk of creating a pessimistic feeling among ensemble members. Smiling, while usually beneficial, is sometimes out of place and can even detrimentally effect the concert mood. Peter Paul Fuchs observes,

> There is nothing more offensive and disillusioning than a conductor who, after the sublimely ethereal final chords of Mahler's *Lied von der Erde,* takes his bow with a broad grin on his face.[4]

2.　Body shielding refers to the act of limiting general body movements and gesturing to practical necessity. Yet anyone who has seen the famous mime Marcel Marceau realizes how expressively communicative the body can be. Partly because of Puritan-based influences, the use of the body for expression other than in dancing has been relatively restricted in our country.

In choral performance this indispensable expressive resource is best employed to *set an example.* Singing posture, physical readiness, and vocal freedom can only be maintained with consistency through our own demonstration.

On a more advanced level the application of physical demonstration transforms the choral director's role into what Wilhelm Ehmann calls a "symbolic dancer." He refers to the importance of keeping alive a sense of "inner dancing" among the members of a choral ensemble. And the author envisions the conductor as a co-participant who "never dances 'the whole dance'. . . . He makes only his hands and his arms dance—the rest of him being kept on the brink of dancing without yielding to the impulse."[5]

---

[4]*The Psychology of Conducting* by Peter Paul Fuchs. © Copyright 1969 by MCA Music, A Division of MCA, Inc., p. 75.
USED BY PERMISSION.　　　　　　　　　　　　ALL RIGHTS RESERVED.

[5]Ehmann, *Choral Directing,* p. 167.

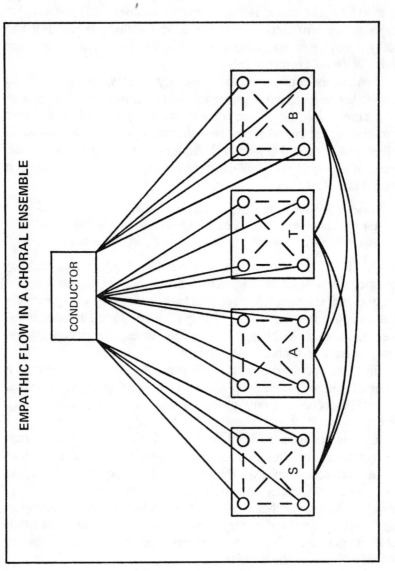

EMPATHIC FLOW IN A CHORAL ENSEMBLE

CONDUCTOR

Figure 1-6

Developing Body Language through Empathic Technique

The word "empathy" was originally used by psychologists and refers to an individual's capacity to understand others through insight and feeling. As a term used by many musicians, it has come to mean:

A feeling of cohesion between the conductor and each performer and among the members of the ensemble.

Empathy can, and should, exist between sections of the ensemble as well. (See Figure 1-6.)

This feeling of cohesion plays an especially important role in choral music because of the unique nature of vocal performance. Only in singing is the musician both the instrument and the performer. And the act of making music vocally requires an intimate blend of psychological and neuro-physical responses. The vocalist sings from the inside out.

In empathizing with our singers, we must learn to stimulate them *through body language* so that they will perform with the proper energizing action necessary to achieve the best vocal result. By working with the ensemble, we must find ways to draw the music out of the performer. One concept which seems particularly helpful in this regard is described as follows:

The choral director should develop the constant image that he is connected by *several* strings with each member of the ensemble. Whenever he moves his hands, arms, or chest, there should be a *physical* feeling of directly controlling the singer's response.

In other words, we must develop an intimate performance rapport with our singers. This link must be established before we make music and is achieved by first looking around at the members to gain eye-to-eye contact.

During the course of performance the competent choral director continually requests desired responses from his singers through body language. Figure 1-7 contains some examples of empathic technique which have proven themselves.

THE CHORAL CONDUCTOR, THE ORCHESTRA, AND THE BATON

Understanding the Orchestral Musician's Environment

The choral director who hopes to work successfully with instrumentalists must learn to communicate with them in a somewhat

---

EMPATHIC TECHNIQUE

Desired Ensemble Result	*Director's Body Language*
Confident entry	Look of expectation
Adequate breath	Open mouth at preparatory beat
Tone support	High chest
Sonority and homogeneity	Firm stance ("center down")
Vocal coloratura	Postural buoyancy
Adequately high intonation	Smile, "weightless conducting"

Figure 1-7

different way than with singers. This difference becomes evident when one considers the orchestral musician's background. The proficient instrumentalist has usually spent many years attempting to master his instrument and learning to sight read. And, as a result of this discipline, he tends to approach performance as an artistic craftsman. Singers also seek technical proficiency, but they are generally more dependent on group motivation and extra-musical factors than their instrumental colleagues.

The orchestral musician usually expects clear, concise instructions and accurate accounting for measures by the conductor. If there is such a thing as "The Golden Rule of Orchestral Conducting," it would undoubtedly be stated as follows:

Always maintain a clear downbeat for every measure!

The history of orchestral performance is full of instances in which wrong entrances occurred because the conductor failed to maintain bar integrity.

Some Guidelines for Directing the Instrumental Ensemble

Competent instrumentalists have learned to count fast and efficiently. Be prepared to work at a relatively faster rehearsal pace. Here are some suggestions.

1. Be ready to offer suggestions to string players about bowing and articulation. Consult a string player, if necessary, for this information.

2. If *potential* trouble spots involve transposing instruments, study these parts closely so that pitch problems can be remedied effectively.

3. For works of extended length use well-placed rehearsal letters rather than measure numbers. Mark the distances from these letters at which important activity occurs.

4. Check instrumentalists' parts for inconvenient page turns and provide additional parts or written-out inserts if necessary.

One of the most challenging problems for those fortunate enough to have the service of a large instrumental ensemble is to remember individual locations of instruments so that they may be properly cued. Usually, instrumental musicians are available for only a few rehearsals just before the concert. One aid which I have found to be particularly useful is the Cue Chart. After determining your seating arrangement for both the singers and the instrumentalists, plot the locations on a piece of cardboard. (See Figure 1-8.) By sitting at a desk with the cue chart positioned behind the score, you can practice cueing and ensure familiarity with locations before actual rehearsals and performances.

The Baton

The controversy of whether or not to use a baton while conducting has persisted for many years. Most arguments on both sides can be narrowed down to the following views:

- The baton offers more clarity and precision than the hand.
- The hand offers more expressive possibilities than the baton.

One way to reach a solution is by asking the musicians themselves which method they prefer. Based on personal experience and discussions with other conductors and ensemble performers, I have found a clear indication that singers usually feel more comfortable with the free hand and instrumentalists prefer the baton unless they are performing in a small chamber group.

I personally take the position that a choral director should become adept at conducting both with and without the baton. By developing a flexibility to conduct either way, you can choose the method which will best fit the situation. This decision should be based on two considerations.

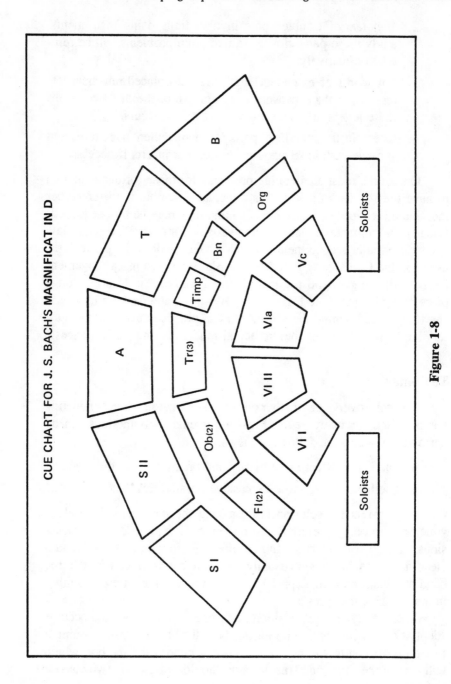

Figure 1-8

1. The chosen method should be determined by the proportion and importance of vocal and instrumental forces required in a particular work. For example, Beethoven's "Choral Symphony" would best be conducted with baton, whereas J.S. Bach's motets, performed with instrumental doubling, would prosper better under the guidance of a free hand.

2. You could elect to employ *both* methods within the same work. This is especially appropriate where a cappella movements are sandwiched between instrumentally accompanied sections. Ralph Vaughan Williams' *Hodie* is an example of such construction.

2

Working with People Who Sing:
How to Use Motivational Techniques

AWARENESS OF THE
INDIVIDUAL AND THE GROUP

Of all the non-musical skills necessary for successful choral directing, the ability to motivate ensemble members toward rehearsal and performance goals is probably the most important. This proficiency is only developed through knowledge of human behavior and practical experience in working with people. Your success will be directly dependent on the following factors:

- Your ability to perceive individual and group needs
- A realistic understanding of your own attributes and limitations as a leader-motivator
- Your insight or feel for human relations
- Your effectiveness in managing interpersonal relationships and influencing human events

The Individual Singer

Choral directors are judged to a large extent by their ability to produce quality ensembles. Sometimes it is possible to forget that organizations are molded from individuals whose efforts and abilities ultimately determine the group's success. Human beings are sensitive to the nature of their leader's persuasion. If manipulated, they can become obstinate; if inspired, they will sacrifice.

As a member of an ensemble the singer has basic needs which must be satisfied. Here are some examples:

1.   The individual seeks to maintain his identity within a group situation. The use of a nickname or preference for unusual or distinctive clothes is evidence of this quest for individuality. New singers are usually preoccupied with achieving a sense of belonging to the group and should be helped to satisfy this immediate goal. An orientation, whether in the form of a short discussion period for each singer or as a formal meeting for an entire contingent of performers, is effective for integrating new members into the choral organization.

Although a sense of individual belonging is important for group success, this does not mean that a "group-think" philosophy should be encouraged. Preoccupation with fitting into the group frustrates individuality. A successful choral ensemble is characterized by a healthy balance between individual identity and group-oriented tasks.

2.   The individual likes to feel that his contribution is necessary for the group's success. Nothing discourages a singer more than to feel that he is "excess baggage" in a vocal ensemble. He must feel important, and importance means responsibility. You can help your members to find satisfaction as contributors in two ways:

- By emphasizing the "link in the chain" theory and challenging all to fulfill their responsibilities
- By personally letting each individual know that his contributions are appreciated ("Thanks for helping me and the group.")

Sometimes it is difficult for a singer to feel his effectiveness as a member of a 150-voice chorus. One way to recognize contribution in such a large organization is by presenting awards for attendance. A close relative of mine lives in Germany and is a faithful member of the local "Liederkranz." During my infrequent visits she shows me, with obvious pride, a gradually increasing collection of attractive glasses awarded for perfect attendance in the singing group.

3.   Individuals are motivated by a hierarchy of unsatisfied needs. Singers join a choral organization because of a *general* need—to sing. However, the amount of motivation varies with each individual depending on the strength of various sub-needs and the chance to satisfy these needs. Here are some hypothetical cases which clarify this point:

- Soprano X was a soloist with her former group before moving into the area. She chose your ensemble because you perform extended works requiring soloists.

- Tenor Y always wanted to sing in a group but never thought he was good enough. He performed a small solo in the last choral concert.

- Alto Z joined an urban choir primarily because it performs regularly with the city's reputable orchestra.

If you can bring the individual's needs close to the group's needs, everyone will benefit. There are two ways to accomplish this goal.

- By knowing the special talents, abilities, and interests of each member and by providing opportunities for them whenever possible

- By "turning members on" to values and benefits inherent in the choral program. This process persuades individuals to adopt *new* personal needs which coincide with group needs

4.   Individuals work better in positive environments. The choral organization depends on the improvement and development of its members for success. Because this growth process involves learning, factors known as reward and punishment come into play. According to the psychologist James Coleman:

> Negative or divergent feedback . . . has the effect of punishment, but its results may vary.
>
> ....
>
> Rewards . . . tend to reinforce what has been learned and to motivate further learning.[1]

Provide a positive environment by following a simple guideline:

Praise frequently; criticize indirectly!

Obviously, a good choral ensemble results from a demanding director. Too much criticism, however, can be discouraging. For example, sarcastic comments may create a cynical attitude among members and even affect tone quality. Group goals can be achieved with enjoyment if you take a positive approach by *encouraging* change.

---

[1]James C. Coleman, *Psychology and Effective Behavior* (Glenview, Illinois: Scott, Foresman and Company, 1969), p. 383.

The Choral Group

Like the individual, the group can be characterized by its patterns of behavior. In fact, much insight can be gained by viewing the organization as a "collective individual."

1. The group has its own personality. This personality is determined by the following factors:

- The organization's customs, beliefs, and values
- The attitudes and motives of its members
- The social structure of the group
- The cohesiveness and morale of the group

You must be receptive and adaptive to the choral ensemble's personality. What works for one group will not necessarily work for another. For example, I learned quickly—and dramatically—that women's glee clubs require a different leadership approach than men's organizations.

This does not mean that the group's nature cannot be changed. A responsible director will always see reason to promote important values and strengthen morale. However, the practical leader will learn to discern between a group's *inherent* traits and its changeable characteristics.

2. The group's energy is affected by patterns of inertia and momentum. Anyone who has faced a tired choral ensemble on the Monday following a busy weekend tour has experienced the effects of group inertia. The reverse effect tends to take place as groups near their goals. Successful football coaches are acutely aware of this ebb-and-flow phenomenon. They attempt to preserve peak efficiency throughout the season by maintaining a demanding training program and by offering incentives such as "the sweet smell of victory."

Groups are also affected by long-range changes in energy. Young, healthy organizations pursue goals enthusiastically. More established groups tend to gravitate toward maintenance of the status quo.

The best way to generate momentum and keep it is to provide *interesting* incentives and goals continually. For example, choose a lighter, novelty piece for the school ensemble's first rehearsal of the spring semester. An established church choir plagued by the duty of having to provide just one more anthem for the Sunday service might pull out of its rut by preparing for a special Saturday night secular concert. Unique concert appearances, unusual repertoire, social events, and even a change in rehearsal location are just a few examples of ways to keep the group on the move.

The Group's View of Its Leader

The organization responds differently to various leaders for many reasons. One of the most important factors in choral ensemble leadership is the director's personality. Yet it is obvious that individuals with completely different life styles and personalities can achieve equally superior results. Organizations are accommodating to a leader as long as he possesses the skills and values sought by that particular group.

Occasionally choral groups place a premium on a leader's values and minimize their concern for his skills. Three years ago I had the opportunity of recommending two potential directors for a large industrial choir. The more musically adept nominee was passed over in favor of a younger neophyte. The latter's promise to provide enjoyable lunchtime recreation proved to be the deciding factor.

While some readers may question that organization's sense of values, the previous example does demonstrate the fact that successful directors, as group leaders, must be prepared to offer more than musical proficiency. Here are some basic functions which you should expect to perform:

- As an organizer, structure the group's environment by providing direction and objectives.
- As a controller of group behavior, point individual interests in the direction of group priorities.
- As a facilitator, help the group reach its goals and potential.

ESTABLISHING A VIABLE RAPPORT

It is the rare individual who can step into a new leadership position and get immediate dramatic results. Usually such changes and improvements require patience and a certain amount of working and growing together between the leader and his group.

Establishing and maintaining a cooperative spirit is especially important in choral performance, because the director and his singers must achieve an unusually sensitive working relationship for performing vocal music. There are three important steps which you can personally take to achieve this rapport.

- Develop an environment conducive to making music.
- Establish necessary guidelines and rules.
- Observe the basic principles of leadership.

Develop an Environment Conducive to Making Music

Individuals join organizations for various reasons, some not always compatible with the main purpose of the group. The classic example of this occurs when church members join choirs so that they may be prominently seen on Sundays. Sometimes the group itself, because of wayward leadership or an unclear sense of values, reaches for its goals in a roundabout way. Several years ago I had the unfortunate experience of replacing a church choir director who liked to "joke and chat" during most of each rehearsal. Needless to say, the quality of performance was mediocre. It took several weeks for me to reestablish a sense of musical purpose.

Your best approach is to make it clear, through verbal communication and through action, that *musical performance* is the nucleus around which the choral program is built. Individual, group, and director interests must be molded and channelled toward that basic activity. (See Figure 2-1.)

To ensure success, minimize distraction and situations unconducive to making music whenever possible. Following are two important suggestions.

1. *Avoid "uptight" situations.* Sometimes tensions result from the pressure of inadequate rehearsal time or differences of opinion. If they are allowed to lead to feelings of hostility, the choral program will suffer. The best way to prevent such conditions is by underplaying the apparent seriousness of the issue involved. There is usually a humorous side to every human situation.

2. *Avoid generalized criticism.* Experienced choral directors have learned that lectures to the group or censure of vocal sections rarely pay off. In such instances, singers do not often accept personal blame. Without losing tact, the director must pinpoint mistakes and make spot corrections. This approach allows everyone to make music with minimum interference.

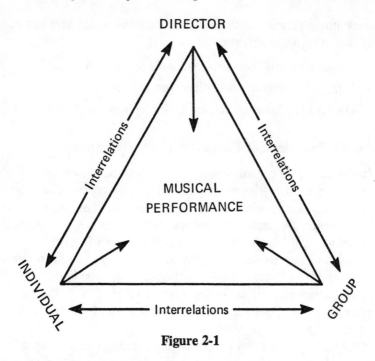

Figure 2-1

Establish Necessary Guidelines and Rules

No organization can exist without the cooperation of its members. To unify and direct this collaborative spirit between individuals, guidelines and rules become necessary. They may be written or assumed or maintained by you or the ensemble's officers, but they must exist.

A viable rapport, which allows the leader and the group to reach for essential objectives, can only be established when all are willing to play the game by its rules. Sociologists have shown that groups need controls *and expect their leaders to provide them.* This does not mean that choral directors should become law enforcement officers; it simply means that healthy individual interests must be directed productively toward group goals.

The exact format and approach for establishing regulatory controls will depend on the nature of the choral organization. A military-oriented academy would tend to adopt a relatively strict code for its glee club members. An adult church choir, on the other hand, will usually respond cooperatively to a verbally presented policy. There are, however, three essential areas of group control which must be clarified for *all* choral ensembles.

1. *Punctuality.* Begin on time and end on time. This policy is based on the assumption that individuals should not be delayed by others. A sixty-voice choral ensemble which begins five minutes late does not lose five minutes. It loses sixty times five minutes or *five manpower hours.*

2. *Absenteeism.* Insist on standards of attendance. I have yet to meet a singer who did not have a good reason for missing a choral rehearsal or performance. The issue is really one of priorities. If an individual misses a rehearsal because of a 103° temperature, one would say that his sense of priority was reasonable. Conversely, if a member is absent from a dress rehearsal because he preferred to watch a televised football game, one would obviously question his choice. The important point of this discussion is contained in the following rule:

> *Insist that choral group members place a proper priority on attendance!*

3. *Attention.* Require active participation and concentration from all members. Individuals rarely come to a rehearsal with the intent of disrupting the group. They *do*, however, like to *talk*. Conversation must be restricted to before and after the rehearsal.

Observe the Basic Principles of Leadership

As previously mentioned, groups respond in different ways to various leaders. But while each choral director must discover which methods and approaches work best for him, he must also keep in mind that a group expects certain basic considerations from its leader. The best way to establish a viable rapport is by observing the following principles of leadership:

1. *Be consistent.* A group cannot follow a straight line toward its goals if the leader vacillates in judgment. For example, if singers are allowed to sit in random order one day and are admonished for this the next day, they become confused and defensive. Yet consistency should be not be confused with inflexibility or stubbornness. The person who refuses to change his decision in the face of contrary evidence is a fool.

2. *Be fair and impartial.* Do not make exceptions. "A chorus cannot tolerate exceptions for individuals: any *prima donna* treatment

signifies the beginning of the end of a genuinely integrated membership."[2] Avoid sectional favoritism or disproportionate criticism of one section over the others. If a choral ensemble is favored by an abundance of good sopranos and plagued by a dearth of tenors (a situation encountered by most directors sooner or later), partiality will obviously polarize the situation.

This discussion is not intended to suggest that individuals or sections should not be acknowledged for superior performance. Rather it means that all must know they have an equal chance to succeed. And the best way to remain fair and impartial is by *challenging* all persons and sections to reach their true potential.

3. *Be reliable.* Group standards will not be met unless the group's leader *sets an example.* How can a director expect his ensemble membership to be punctual if he is not? The old expression, "Do as I say, not as I do," is the banal code of inferior leaders and reflects a calloused indifference to followers.

4. *Be loyal.* Loyalty works both ways. If the group feels that its leader cares and is willing to fight for its cause, support will grow for the leader. Loyalty also means sharing the credits for success. Choral directors sometimes receive letters praising well-received performances; as a matter of professional policy, these notes should be read to the ensemble, followed by a personal "thank you."

5. *Be decisive.* The ability to solve problems and make decisions is not always easy to acquire, but it is a responsibility of leadership. Groups may like "nice guys," but they respect decision-makers. Only several days ago I was faced with the task of choosing members for a select university chamber choir. Of those singers returning for audition, two were not asked to rejoin the group. This decision was based on a preference for two more-talented freshmen and a desire to maintain a continual flow of new members. Although the "retired" singers expressed personal disappointment, members in the newly formed chamber choir have already begun to establish a tighter rapport and perform better than last year's group.

6. *Keep everyone informed.* No one likes to be "left out in the cold" about group plans and activities. Obviously, individuals will work better toward group objectives if they are continually kept abreast of all decisions which affect them. Some people are more resistant to

---

[2]Kurt Thomas, *The Choral Conductor.* Translated by Alfred Mann and William H. Reese. (New York: Associated Music Publishers, 1971), p. 43.

change than others. By supplying them with background about decisions, such as factors considered or reasons for a choice, you can help these individuals in their readjustment.

LEADERSHIP DEVELOPMENT

A leader is able to influence followers through the power of authority. This authorization is usually assumed or granted spontaneously by the group, but it always exists. Behavioral scientists inform us that there are three types of leadership authority.

1. Traditional—based on the *position* filled by the leader. For example, a choral director working within the jurisdiction of a school has traditional authority as a teacher.
2. Functional—based on the leader's *expertise*. This type of authority is stronger because it is related to the leader's competence in his field.
3. Personal—based on the *personality* and social influence of the leader. This form of authority is best because it promotes a cooperative spirit from the group members.

Obviously, a leader who possesses all three types of authority will have the best potential for motivating people and achieving results. Put in simpler language, this means that an appointed choral director who can combine musical skill with "friendly persuasion" will probably be the most successful.

Achieving Personal Authority

The ability to elicit willing responses from others is largely dependent on one's personality. David Ewen, in discussing the characteristics of a good conductor, considers ". . . a magnetic personality as important to a conductor as scholarship, and much more essential than either perfect pitch or a photographic memory.[3]

Personality is determined by fairly permanent characteristics, but it can always be improved. Here are some helpful suggestions, guaranteed to help you become a better motivator.

---

[3]David Ewen, *Dictators of the Baton* (Chicago: Ziff-Davis Publishing Company, 1943), p. 9.

1.   Develop *and maintain* a wholesome, cheerful outlook on life, people, and music. Groups respond to enthusiastic leaders. And enthusiasm is generated by optimism. Sometimes rehearsal pressures can cause a certain amount of anxiety or hostility. Too many of these frustrations cause "job tarnish." Three important rules can help minimize negative reactions.

- Do not take things too personally.
- Try to find some sense of humor in all situations.
- Develop an ability to bounce back from unpleasant incidents.

The only way to maintain optimism is by cultivating a positive manner and viewpoint. Positiveness is also the most natural way to gain confidence and to develop self-control for working with people who sing. The ability to see inherent good in self and others will mark the difference between a director who "fills a slot" and a dynamic leader.

2.   Develop a penchant for flexibility and vitality. Nothing is more ironic than an eager choral group held back by a dead-weight director. The energetic leader is always looking for ways to avoid rehearsal staleness or numbed interpersonal relationships. His interest in group vitality demands concern for his own personal health and physical condition.

To maintain flexibility, you will need to guard against mental ruts. Procrustean thinking, commonly called "putting square pegs in round holes," leads to petrification. There *are* other works suitable for Easter besides Handel's "Hallelujah Chorus," especially when the choir sopranos cannot reach the high A.

3.   Cultivate patience and tact. In working with people who sing, always strive to achieve a compatible relationship with the conditions and moods of your performers. Max Rudolf, in discussing rehearsal techniques, makes the following observation:

> A flair for what to say, and what not to say, is part of a conductor's psychological perception and calls for presence of mind. To know how to word criticisms, to feel when to give encouragement, to sense when a tense moment is best relieved by a joking remark, all this affects the relationship between the leader and his group.[4]

---

[4]Max Rudolf, "Rehearsal Techniques," *The Conductor's Art*, ed. by Carl Bamberger (New York: McGraw-Hill Book Company, 1965), pp. 290-91.

Sometimes problems work themselves out better if treated gently rather than with force. Patient understanding does have its virtue, especially when applied to artistic endeavor. And the director who has not learned to get his ego out of the way in uptight situations will be unable to develop that unique quality called graciousness.

4. Be an idealist. In spite of admonitions to be practical by the world's pragmatists, there will always be leaders who, through a desire for something better than life's mediocrity, will bring untold happiness and success to others. The point is, one can be an idealist *and* a realist if ways can be found to transform ideals into attainable goals. Groups are only inspired by leaders with inspiration. And ideals convey a feeling of purpose and a sense of progress.

GROUP DYNAMICS—THE KEY TO SUCCESS

Anyone who follows the progress of baseball or football teams knows that it is possible to have good coaches and talented players but still not be able to come up with a winning team. Organizations must "put it all together" if they are to succeed. The procedure for attaining this coordinated group effort is called group dynamics. According to sociologists, three conditions or stages are necessary.

- Stage 1—Organizational Self-Motivation
- Stage 2—Organizational Cohesion
- Stage 3—Organizational Morale

Organizational Self-Motivation

Individuals tend to achieve more as members of a group. Groups, in turn, tend to accomplish more when they are allowed to participate in decision making. Scientific studies show that work output, interest, responsibility, originality, and friendliness are greater when a group's leader practices a democratic rather than an authoritarian or laissez-faire form of leadership behavior.

Choral directing does not always lend itself well to this type of guidance. In many instances you will have to make arbitrary decisions. But it is because of this situation that you should make a continual effort to consult the ensemble's officers and members whenever possible. During rehearsals try the self-motivation approach by playing the role of a catalyst, releasing energies that already exist in the group. For example, rather than criticizing an ensemble for poor performance, ask the following questions:

- Were you satisfied with your performance?
- Why was the performance inferior?
- What suggestions do you have for improvement?

The responses are always sincere. Sometimes they lead to intense individual involvement and personal commitment. In several instances I have been requested to schedule extra rehearsals by choral members.

Organizational Cohesion

As individuals begin to feel a sense of belonging, cohesiveness occurs. The relative strength of this togetherness is determined by the attraction the group has for its members. A highly cohesive situation brings about what is commonly known as esprit de corps. The result of such a close-knit feeling is coordinated effort and action. According to James Coleman, groups imbued with a sense of teamwork,

> . . . tend to develop characteristic ways of doing things and, con-currently, strong feelings that these are the ways things *should* be done—that these are the "normal" ways, the "right" ways.[5]

Cohesion is very important for a singing organization.

- It gives the ensemble a sense of identity.
- It encourages mutual confidence and loyalty between the membership and the director.
- It promotes a stronger cooperative spirit.

Learn to encourage team spirit so that singers can be mobilized toward key group goals. Here are some suggestions:

- Develop standard procedures which are worthy of becoming traditions.
- Encourage the sharing of common values.
- Emphasize the importance of individual responsibility to the group.

---

[5]James C. Coleman, *Psychology and Effective Behavior* (Glenview, Illinois: Scott, Foresman and Company, 1969), p. 278.

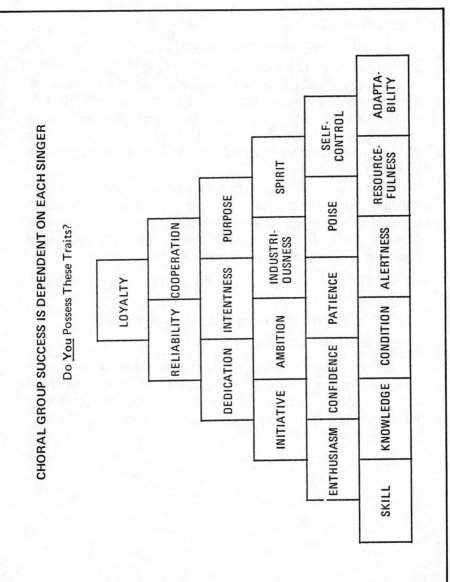

Figure 2-2

• Stimulate individuals through objective demands tied into acknowledged group goals.

Organizational Morale

Morale develops only as a result of cohesion and can best be described as a prevailing mood of confidence in the group's ability to cope with problems. This collective mental condition is achieved when the organization shows a willingness to accept discipline and endure hardship. Only through a strong sense of group spirit can the choral ensemble move toward artistic refinement and musical growth. Standards may be established as a result of cohesiveness, but they will only be met as a result of morale.

Morale is the driving force behind human action. It reaches its ultimate stage when members of the group become convinced that everyone is striving together for something more important than self. You can best instill morale by establishing a competitive spirit among your singers and by providing incentives. For example:

• The ensemble can be challenged to perform better than last year.
• The group can be compared with similar ensembles.
• Individuals can compete for solos.

Sometimes high morale can be encouraged by showing singers how their basic commitments and personal attributes will affect the success of the organization. A very effective way is to provide new members with a Choral Group Success Chart. (See Figure 2-2.)

3

Objectives for Professional Growth

CHORAL DIRECTING
DEMANDS CONTINUAL ASSESSMENT

Unlike dead-end jobs, which often force individuals to repeat a small repertoire of skills, choral directing requires diversification and growth. Even in choral situations hampered by such restrictions as an insensitive administration or limited funds, the enterprising director will usually find ways to build a quality choral program. It is safe to assume that almost all top-notch vocal organizations got that way despite their inadequacies and because of dynamic leadership.

As obvious as it may seem, it is easy to forget that the first step necessary to solve a problem is to recognize that the problem does, in fact, exist. For choral directors this means honestly assessing our repertoire of skills and knowledge for weaknesses and "rust spots." Here are two factors to keep in mind:

- There is a big difference between prerequisite qualification and real effectiveness. Beginning choral directors who have received training in basic conducting skills can be compared with young army officers—they are equipped merely to survive the battle.
- Growth is continuous, but it requires the sacrifice of sedateness. On the other hand, development is an essential component of true professionalism.

Evaluating Musical Skills and Knowledge

Besides conducting with facility, you must learn to manage an array of associated but integral musical skills and knowledge. These musical "components" can be classified according to their type of activity and their level of difficulty. The Taxonomy of Choral Skills and Knowledge represents a highly systematized classification of these musical responsibilities. If you will rate your ability for each sub-category, strengths and deficiencies will become immediately apparent. The Taxonomy is a unique guide for self-improvement.

TAXONOMY OF CHORAL SKILLS AND KNOWLEDGE
(Excluding Conducting Skills)

I. SKILLS

In each of the following five skill categories, rate yourself on each skill as follows: cannot perform, poor, fair, good, or excellent.

A.   SINGING

	Sub-Categories
1.	Sing in tune
2.	Sing with tonal control
3.	Sing with technical proficiency
4.	Sing with stylistic diversification
5.	Sing with musical expression

B.   VOCAL SIGHT READING

	Sub-Categories
1.	Sing own vocal line
2.	Sing various vocal lines in treble and bass clefs
3.	Sing individual lines in keyboard accompaniment
4.	Sing individual instrumental lines in various clefs

C.   KEYBOARD PLAYING

	Sub-Categories
1.	Accompany warm-up exercises
2.	Play individual vocal lines in treble and bass clefs
3.	Play combined vocal lines in closed score
4.	Play combined vocal lines in open score
5.	Play keyboard accompaniment for score study
6.	Play keyboard accompaniment in rehearsals
7.	Play keyboard accompaniment in performances
8.	Play combined instrumental lines in open score

D.	LISTENING
	Sub-Categories
1.	Hear faulty intonation
2.	Hear incorrect notes in melodic line
3.	Hear incorrect notes within harmonic structure
4.	Hear incorrect dynamic levels
5.	Hear faulty phrasing
6.	Hear improper blend
7.	Hear improper balance
8.	Hear incorrect articulation

E.	RHYTHMIC PERCEPTION
	Sub-Categories
1.	Choose proper tempos
2.	Maintain steady tempos
3.	Hear incorrect rhythms
4.	Sense underlying pulsation and stress
5.	Have feel for rhythmic deviations such as syncopation and hemiola

F.	DICTION
	Sub-Categories
1.	Pronounce English texts with precision
2.	Pronounce foreign texts with precision
3.	Detect inaccuracies in ensemble diction
4.	Translate foreign texts for essential meaning

G.	SILENT SCORE STUDY
	Sub-Categories
1.	Hear individual vocal lines
2.	Hear combined vocal lines
3.	Hear keyboard accompaniment
4.	Hear combined instrumental lines
5.	Hear harmonic progressions and key changes

II. KNOWLEDGE

In each of the following five knowledge categories rate yourself in each area as follows: do not know, poor, fair, good, or excellent.

A. TERMINOLOGY AND SYMBOLS
Sub-Categories

1.	Know terms and symbols for tempos
2.	Know terms and symbols for dynamics
3.	Know expressive terms and symbols
4.	Know articulation terms and symbols
5.	Know designations and abbreviations for instruments

B. SCORE MECHANICS
Sub-Categories

1.	Understand directions for movement through the score (repeats, endings, and so on)
2.	Know usual locations of choral parts and instrumental families within score
3.	Know intervals of transposition for pertinent instruments

C. THEORETICAL INSIGHT
Sub-Categories

1.	Locate keys (or tonal structure) and modulations
2.	Analyze form
3.	Locate melodic, harmonic, and rhythmic tension and release
4.	Identify characteristics which give the work its specific identity

D. CHORAL HISTORY AND REPERTOIRE
Sub-Categories

1.	Understand relative importance of composers in perspective
2.	Know their choral works
3.	Know quality works by lesser known composers
4.	Have grasp of choral repertoire in various stylistic periods, for various accompanying forces, and for various types of choral ensembles

E. PERFORMANCE PRACTICE
Sub-Categories

1.	Know the expressive possibilities of various types of voices
2.	Know the expressive possibilities and limitations of the various instruments, including organ
3.	Understand basic concepts and traditions for performing music from all stylistic periods

Pursuing Avenues of Growth

As was previously pointed out, several non-musical roles are necessary for effective choral direction. Obviously, if these duties were broken down into general skills and knowledge and added to the Taxonomy of Choral Skills and Knowledge, we would have an impressive checklist of things to do throughout our choral directing lifetime.

The question is: how can we begin to satisfy these professional requirements? The answer is: by pursuing three main avenues of learning and experience:

- Self-accumulated skills and knowledge. This is gradually accomplished through individual practice and direct access to information in books and other reference materials.
- Guidance and consultation. Other choral directors, teachers, and non-musical specialists are sought for needed improvement, clarification, and further information.
- Performance opportunities. General musicianship as well as conducting skills are sharpened through individual, chamber, and larger ensemble performing experiences. This also includes music making in non-choral fields.

The remainder of this chapter deals with concrete ways to pursue these avenues of growth.

ESTABLISHING A PERSONAL RESOURCE CENTER

Because choral direction is a pragmatically oriented activity, vocal leaders usually need information and facility for getting into their music quickly. You may partly depend on school music libraries, departmental listening equipment, or the church organ, but the best solution is to establish and develop a personal resource center for such purposes. This "operations center" should include the following resources:

- Reference books
- Professional information
- Music publishers' catalogues and printed music

- Record and tape library
- Instruments and equipment

Reference Books

Begin by establishing a nucleus of books which provide essential information. The following list constitutes a *basic* library which should be augmented whenever possible:

1. Conducting and directing

   Harold Decker and Julius Herford, editors. *Choral Conducting: A Symposium*. Appleton-Century-Crofts, 1973.

   Wilhelm Ehmann. *Choral Directing*. Translated by George Wiebe. Augsburg Publishing House, 1968.

   Elizabeth Green. *Conducting*. 2nd ed. Prentice-Hall, 1969.

   Kurt Thomas. *The Choral Conductor*. Translated by Alfred Mann and William H. Reese. Associated Music Publishers, 1971.

2. Voice

   Victor Fields. *Training the Singing Voice*. King's Crown Press (a subsidiary of Columbia University Press), 1966.

   Arnold Rose. *The Singer and the Voice.* St. Martin's Press, 1971.

   William Vennard. *Singing, the Mechanism and the Technic*. Carl Fischer, 1967.

3. Diction

   Evelina Colorni. *Singers' Italian*. G. Schirmer, 1970.

   Richard Cox. *The Singer's Manual of German and French Diction*. G. Schirmer, 1970.

   Madeleine Marshall. *The Singer's Manual of English Diction*. G. Schirmer, 1953.

4. Choral repertoire

   Charles Burnsworth. *Choral Music for Women's Voices*. Scarecrow Press, 1968.

   Choral Music in Print. Musicdata (Philadelphia), 1974.

Merrill Knapp. *Selected List of Music for Men's Voices.* Princeton University Press, 1952.

Arthur Locke and Charles Fassett. *Selected List of Choruses for Women's Voices.* Smith College, 1964.

William Tortolano. *Original Music for Men's Voices.* Scarecrow Press, 1973.

5. Choral history and literature

Arthur Jacobs, editor. *Choral Music.* Pelican Books, 1963.

Homer Ulrich. *A Survey of Choral Music.* Harcourt Brace Jovanovich, 1973.

Percy Young. *The Choral Tradition.* Hutchinson (London), 1963.

6. General music history

Richard Crocker. *A History of Musical Style.* McGraw-Hill, 1966.

Donald Grout. *A History of Western Music.* Revised ed. W. W. Norton, 1973.

7. Stylistic interpretation

Thurston Dart. *The Interpretation of Music.* Harper and Row, 1963.

Robert Donington. *The Interpretation of Early Music.* Faber and Faber (London), 1963.

8. Music theory

Jan La Rue. *Guidelines for Style Analysis.* W. W. Norton, 1970.

Walter Piston. *Harmony.* 3rd ed. W. W. Norton, 1969.

Felix Salzer and Carl Schachter. *Counterpoint in Composition.* McGraw-Hill, 1969.

9. Acoustics

John Backus. *The Acoustical Foundations of Music.* W. W. Norton, 1969.

10. Terminology

Willi Apel. *Harvard Dictionary of Music.* 2nd ed. Harvard University Press, 1970.

Professional Information

What pitfalls should be avoided when you are preparing for a European tour? What are some of the characteristics found in Charles Ives' choral music? These are the types of questions answered by choral periodicals. In this country, there are presently two important professional publications:

The Choral Journal
Published by the American Choral Directors Association
P.O. Box 17736
Tampa, Florida 33612

American Choral Review
Published by the American Choral Foundation
130 West 56th Street
New York, New York 10019

All issues received should be saved for future reference. I have often found valuable information contained in old copies that I thought were merely serving as dust catchers.

Who will furnish red octavo music folders in a hurry? Where can one purchase lightweight risers? Merchandising catalogues and advertisements provide this kind of information. Like choral periodicals, they will eventually prove their value if they are saved and stored for ready access.

Publishers' Catalogues and Printed Music

Choral catalogues and music are often collected in a haphazard way. The trouble with this approach is that there is little control over the scope or quality of available literature. Here is a sure-fire method for building and maintaining a substantial choral library:

1.   Do not depend on publishers to find you; write to them for catalogues. Also don't overlook music *distributors* who offer their own catalogues covering music published by others. Here are two excellent clearing houses:

J. W. Pepper
P.O. Box 850
Valley Forge, Pennsylvania 19482

Joseph Boonin
P.O. Box 2124
South Hackensack, New Jersey 07606

2. Write for reference copies of music from publishers. If possible, use stationery with your organization's letterhead, and be sure that these firms know that you are the choral director. As a rule of thumb, request courtesy copies whenever you assume a new position or plan to establish a new ensemble. Also include this information in your letter.

3. Pull reference copies of music from your present organization's choral library. Nothing is more wasteful than to order new music only to discover later that this music was actually on hand.

4. Store music properly. Use a music cabinet with shallow shelves, or build one yourself. Music should then be categorized according to scoring, type of composition, and potential use. Music under immediate consideration or in actual use should, of course, be kept separately.

Record and Tape Library

There is no such thing as a definitive collection of choral recordings, because new discs as well as professional and non-commercial tapes are made almost every day. There are, however, guidelines which you should use in establishing and maintaining your personal collection.

1. Keep abreast of latest releases through record and tape guides rather than relying on perusal through a store's current inventory. Two publications of particular importance are:

Schwann Record and Tape Guide
Available monthly in record shops

Annual Catalogue
The Musical Heritage Society
1991 Broadway
New York, New York 10023

2. Formulate a priority strategy for developing that type of collection which best meets your needs. Here are some suggestions:

- Choose the "choral monuments" first as a nucleus for the library.
- Locate recordings of music you are most likely to use. Your chances of performing music which employs limited or no accompaniment are probably greater than your chances of performing works requiring full orchestra.

- Search for works using contrasting scoring, such as compositions for men's voices, music for voices and strings, and so on.
- Choose recordings of music from various stylistic periods, written for different purposes. It is easy to find sacred Baroque choral performances, for example, but a balanced collection would include court music as well.

3. Initiate an index card file system.

- File each work on a record or tape recording under the composer's name.
- Assign locator numbers to discs and tapes as they are added to your collection.

4. Do not overlook amateur recordings of live performances. Commercial record companies have neglected important choral works, especially shorter compositions. Some of my most valuable tape recordings have come from live radio broadcasts and from friends' concerts.

Instruments and Equipment

Most church and school choral directors rely heavily on keyboard instruments provided at their places of work. School musicians also depend on their schools' listening equipment. Yet professional directors usually need to plan and work on their own time. Much can be accomplished in the privacy of your residence if it is properly equipped. A model resource center would include the following items:

1. Music reading equipment
- Keyboard instrument
- Metronome

2. Listening equipment
- Record player
- Tape recorder
- Additional tape recorder for duplication of tapes
- AM-FM radio tuner and amplifier (or receiver)

- Speakers
- Earphones
3. Administrative equipment
- Storage facilities for music, books, records, tapes, and catalogues
- Desk and lamp
- Typewriter
- Music stand
- Full-length mirror
- Planning calendar and bulletin board
- Office supplies

WAYS TO ACCUMULATE FACTS, INSIGHTS, AND SKILLS

Attending Workshops, Conventions, and Courses

Competent choral directors actively seek help from others. Workshops and conventions are typical avenues for improvement. For example, the American Choral Directors Association sponsors state workshops as well as district and national conventions. Activities include special topic sessions led by reputable choral specialists and concerts performed by excellent ensembles. Often much insight develops out of informal "rap sessions" between directors talking shop during their leisure.

Colleges and universities have come a long way in offering more specialized courses for the established choral director. What conductor would not benefit by seeing an instant replay of his technique on videotape or by taking a refresher course in choral repertoire? Not to be overlooked are non-music courses in such areas as social psychology and management.

Attending Concerts

The choral director who does not find the time to attend concerts endangers his chances of growth, for only through attending concerts can he begin to see his own efforts in perspective. Besides hearing new repertoire, the visiting director can compare interpretations, methods of programming, and quality of ensemble response.

Attending non-choral performances by professional musicians is also important, primarily because these concerts help to provide general standards of quality and aesthetic inspiration. Here are two suggestions which I have found to be personally useful:

1. Attend rehearsals as well as performances and sit close to the director. You will learn much about gesture, communication, and working rapport.

2. Watch televised presentations of major orchestra concerts on the National Educational Network. Camera coverage of these performances provides unique views of world-renown conductors.

Performing

It is unfortunate that some choral directors become numbed to music's expressive qualities because they have partially lost contact with their own art. Personal involvement in active music making, aside from conducting, is the best defense against musical insensitivity. There are two available avenues of performance, each providing separate rewards.

1. Performing as a soloist will help you to "sharpen up" your talents, abilities, and overall musicianship. The process of preparing for a recital also has many correlations with group preparation.

2. Singing in a choral ensemble may sound like a "busman's holiday," but it provides you the opportunity to re-experience the problems and responsibilities which your choristers encounter. In better choral groups, it also offers the chance to experience interdependence between vocal and accompanying forces. There are also two secondary reasons for performing in choral ensembles.

- Proficiency in score reading is developed.
- Other directors are observed under fire.

BROADENING PERSPECTIVE

Continual growth as a choral director requires keeping up with a vide range of new ideas and innovations. Here are some examples:

- New music
- Early period music published in performance editions for the first time
- Techniques for teaching contemporary music
- Concepts for improving diction and tone quality
- New audio-visual aids

Growth also means dynamic movement from a grasp of basic choral skills to more general musical competencies. For example, understanding music history will give you a perspective about composers and a sense of direction in looking for repertoire. Have you ever heard of Luca Marenzio or Giacomo Gastoldi? These Renaissance musicians produced some of the finest choral works of all time, and their music is readily available.

Finally, growth means improvement in non-musical tasks and activities. Finding better ways to work with people who sing and learning to organize one's own administrative functions more efficiently are prime examples.

This last point brings to mind an actual example. A very competent colleague recently told me that she had received a flattering compliment from a student. The choir member informed her that she was especially appreciated by the ensemble because she "cared for the students" and because she "had interests in other areas besides choral music." I would say that this is an individual with broadened perspective.

4

Establishing a Quality Choral
Program: Planning and Promotion

GROUP PURPOSE MUST BE DEFINED

Politicians who promise something for everyone are often criticized for their inability to take a stand where it counts. So it is with choral groups attempting to be all things to all people. Let's face it: some ensembles perform Bach better than Bacharach and vice versa. Therefore, one of your primary responsibilities is to determine what your particular group can do best and then pursue that course of action. When I directed a rural college choir I was occasionally asked why the ensemble did not perform "lighter" music in its annual Christmas programs. My answer was a simple one: "Because other choral groups in the area already provide that service." I would then point out that this college choir was one of the few local groups capable of performing classical music with proficiency.

Situational Circumstances

Quite often the major role of a vocal ensemble is predetermined by certain permanent conditions. The following examples illustrate this point:

- A new church expects its budding choir to sing an anthem every Sunday.
- Members of an ethnic chorus usually meet for the purpose of performing music from their culture.

Figure 4-1 clearly presents those situational circumstances which tend to control or at least influence a large part of a choral group's basic nature. If applicable factors are selected from each category, the general purpose of a particular vocal organization becomes evident. Note, however, that more than one factor can be chosen from each category.

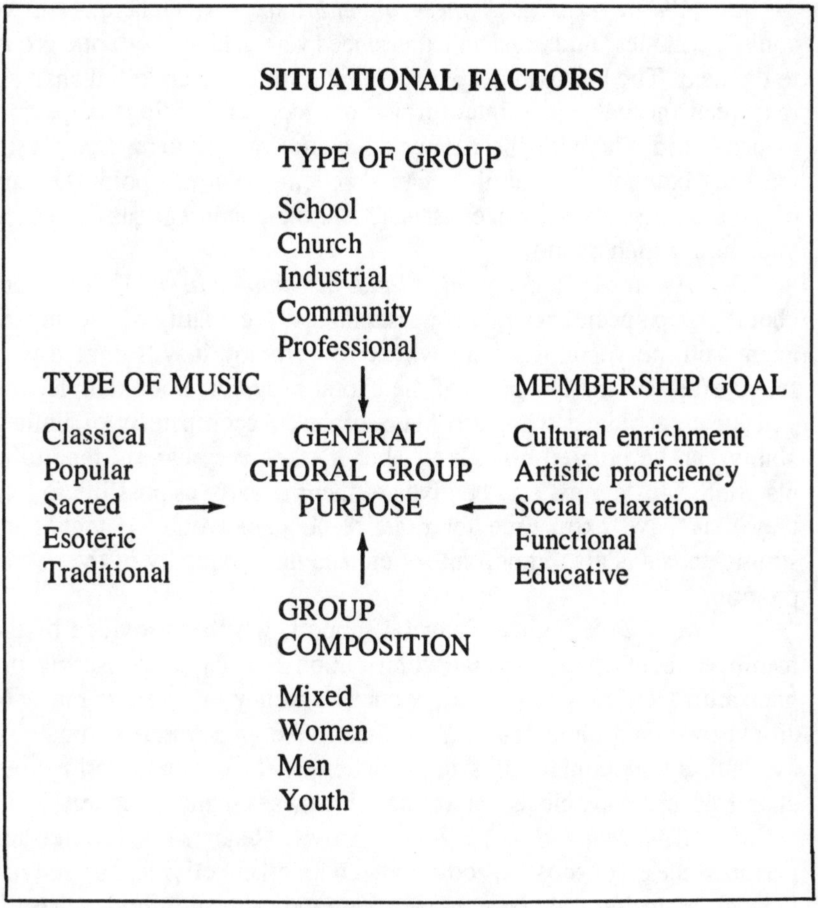

SITUATIONAL FACTORS

TYPE OF GROUP

School
Church
Industrial
Community
Professional

TYPE OF MUSIC		MEMBERSHIP GOAL
Classical	GENERAL	Cultural enrichment
Popular	CHORAL GROUP	Artistic proficiency
Sacred ⟶	PURPOSE ⟵	Social relaxation
Esoteric		Functional
Traditional		Educative

GROUP COMPOSITION

Mixed
Women
Men
Youth

Figure 4-1

Making Preliminary Estimates

Once you have an idea about the group's overall purpose, the next step is to look around to see what resources are available. It is also important at this point to find out how the choral program relates to other activities as well as how it best fits within the general environment. The following estimates will provide you with a comprehensive picture:

1. *Probable number of interested singers.* A small high school may have difficulty in maintaining a sizeable choral program unless musical participation has been built up over the years. On the other hand, a large university can support several quality choral ensembles.

2. *Characteristics of these potential singers.* General level of ability, attitudes, and musical experiences vary widely from one group to the next. The best way for a new director to make an initial analysis is to read through old printed programs, locate recordings of performances, and talk with the former conductor and singers. Some estimate of potential vocal abilities can also be made at this point. Do any of the students receive voice lessons? Are there any real bass voices at your junior high school?

3. *Available accompanists and instrumentalists.* Unless your choral group specializes in a cappella music, the quality of accompaniment and the versatility with which you employ it will have a profound effect on the character of the choral program. For example, can you locate a pianist who also plays organ? Accompanists of limited ability can be utilized effectively, but it takes very careful repertoire planning. Music must also be given to them as early as possible so that they may have extra time for practice. Locating other potential instrumentalists is also important for enhancing the quality of the choral program.

4. *Available funds.* Financial support, whether provided by the members themselves, through contributions, or by a sponsoring organization, will range from barely enough money to purchase music to all-expense-paid choir tours. You must make an accurate estimate of available and potential funds and then be realistic enough to bring your choral group plans closely into line with these financial figures.

5. *Conflicts with other organizations.* Rehearsal schedules and performance dates must be coordinated with other activities, or you run the risk of losing members as well as good faith with colleagues. If conflicts are unavoidable, compromises must be made. Making a satisfactory estimate means tracking down the schedules of all organizations and lists of special events and then attempting to fit the choral program within this picture to create minimal conflict.

6. *Administrative restrictions.* School choral directors quickly become adept at scheduling concerts and rehearsals around the

school's yearly calendar. Church choir leaders are restricted by seasonal changes in worship. One does not, for example, perform Lotti's *Crucifixus* during advent. It generally pays to consult administrators, clergymen, or others responsible for guidance in working out your plans.

SELLING THE PROGRAM AND CHOOSING MEMBERS

Locating potential singers and "turning them on" to the advantages of performing in your choral group is one of the most important ingredients for establishing a quality choral program. Without singers there will be no choir, and without the best available performers the organization can't reach its true potential.

Spreading the Word

The first step in locating possible members is to use whatever avenues of communication are necessary to reach them. School students are accessible through a few strategically placed posters and the school bulletin. Community choral groups, on the other hand, depend on newspaper announcements and telephone calls for their success. It is always a good idea to saturate the market by using as many modes of communication as possible. Here are some further examples.

- Public announcements in classes, at meetings, in dining halls, and so on
- Mailed notices
- Radio announcements
- Word of mouth through members
- Audition information provided at the bottom of printed programs

The actual information you choose to provide these potential singers, as well as the way in which it is presented, is very important because, in effect, you are attempting to "sell" the choral program. Obviously, such basic facts as the time and place for auditions need to be stated, but other appealing information should be included. Some comment about an exciting choral work to be performed or an interesting upcoming performance is always helpful. (See Figure 4-2.)

JOIN THE COLBY-SAWYER CONCERT CHOIR!

_____

Sing with the Dartmouth Glee Club

* * * * *

Travel to Boston and perform in historic Old North Church

_____

AUDITIONS FOR NEW MEMBERS

Tuesday, February 18 and Wednesday, February 19

7—9 p.m.   *   Gordon Hall   *   Sawyer Center

Figure 4-2

Do not overlook the best sales pitch available for an established choral group—an extra performance at audition time. Returning students can put together a short effective work or two, especially if it was included in their previous repertoire, and the sound of music combined with a few comments by the director will do much to lure new singers into auditions.

Sometimes individuals who would secretly like to sing in your non-selective ensemble need a little extra coaxing. Whenever I announced a need for new members in my volunteer church choir, I always made the following concluding remark: "We are not looking for singers; we are just looking for people who like to sing."

Setting up the Auditions

The purpose of the audition is to determine the prospective member's talent and ability with minimum red tape and maximum tactfulness. Long lines and unanswered questions create disgruntled singers; smooth-running procedures and human sensitivity pave the way for maximum responsiveness. The following suggestions will help to ensure successful auditions:

1.   If many singers are involved, set up a time schedule to minimize waiting time. Here are three alternatives.

- Post a sign-up time sheet prior to the audition day.
- Provide time cards at the audition. Those with later times may leave and return.
- Find out ahead of time who will audition and assign times in advance.

2.   Hold auditions privately. This helps to alleviate nervousness and allows for a more personalized audition.

3.   Provide information about the group to be read by singers before they enter the audition. Include the following data:

- Rehearsal schedule
- Concert schedule
- Course credit, fees, and so on, if applicable
- Regulations
- Repertoire to be performed
- Anticipated size of the group

4.   Post a brief outline of the actual audition procedure. This helps prevent confusion. Also include information about how and when those selected will be notified.

5.   Keep the auditions running smoothly by using an assistant. Make sure this individual knows as much about the choral program as you do so that questions may be effectively answered.

6.   Use audition forms and have singers fill them out before entering the audition. This not only saves valuable time, it also provides a permanent record. (See Figure 4-3.)

Determining Audition Procedures

The actual audition may include simply having the singer perform a short song or sing several scales to administering intensive diagnostic tests in sight reading and musical memory. The choice of ingredients will be based on two important factors:

1.   *Level of selectivity.* How critical will you be when choosing new choir members? A small school with several conflicting activities might require you to choose a low level of selectivity and "take what

AUDITION FORM

Name_____
          last   first

Class_____

Dorm or local address_____
_____
_____

Phone_____

Previous choir experience____
_____

Soloist experience_____
_____

List any instruments you
play _____
_____
_____

Name and location of
high school attended_____
_____

Do not write in this space

Range_____

Quality_____

Intonation_____

Sight reading_____
       _____

Concert Choir_____

Chamber Singers_____
       _____

Soloist_____

Section leader_____

Accompanist_____
       _____

Comments_____

Figure 4-3

you can get.'' Conversely, a semi-professional chamber ensemble would require fairly selective auditions. With large turn-outs of singers, time can be saved by holding *two* auditions. The first serves the purpose of quickly screening candidates for those with superior qualifications. The second audition is more selective.

    2. *Criteria for examination.* After deciding the level of selectiv-

ity, you must consider exactly what it is you hope to discover about the auditioner. If the standards for acceptance into the vocal organization are minimal, you would probably only be interested in finding out if the individual can carry a tune. You would also need to know his vocal range. On the other hand, high selectivity would require you to consider such details as vocal agility and enunciation. Here is a comprehensive list of possible criteria for examination.

- Intonation—melodic, harmonic
- Range—extremes, tessitura
- Tone quality—color, clarity, weight
- Vocal control—agility, vibrato, dynamics
- Diction—vowel clarity, consonant clarity
- Sight reading—rhythm, pitch
- Musicality—phrasing, textural awareness, general fluency

Constructing an Audition Test

Devising a format for auditioning is a highly personal task based on past experiences and general knowledge about the singers. Here is a procedure which I have found to work best for moderately selective auditions.

1.   Have the auditioner sing a well-known song. Play only harmonic accompaniment to see if he can sustain the melodic line. Ask the singer to perform the song again emphasizing diction and interpretation.

2.   Vocalize the auditioner up and down a five-note scale passage, modulating each exercise upward until the highest comfortable note is reached. Reverse this process by inverting the scale passage and modulating downward until the lowest comfortable note is reached. See how much these vocalizations can be performed without piano. Some singers will require a chord at each successive modulation; others will make the changes themselves.

3.   Have the auditioner sight read his voice part in unknown four-part songs (perhaps composed by you). These should be graduated in difficulty and accompanied (excluding the singer's part) so that he can perform his part contextually. If he stumbles, allow a second chance to see if mistakes are corrected. This sight reading

procedure is more relevent than confronting the singer with unaccompanied note patterns.

Considering Non-Musical Criteria

Sometimes the most talented singer or the best sight reader turns out to be a mediocre ensemble member. Experienced choral leaders often discover that individuals with strong interest and dedication accomplish more for a group than others with more musical ability. Two factors should be considered in this regard.

1. *Intelligence.* Being a responsive and alert chorister takes brainpower. The individual with the greater capacity for perceiving relationships and thinking conceptually can respond faster and more thoroughly. All other factors being equal, take the more intelligent auditioner.

Not necessarily related to intelligence, but also important, is academic average. Most membership turnover not related to graduation can be attributed to students having difficulty with courses. Quite often these students decide to spend more time with their books and begin looking for ways to increase study time. Guess which activity "gets the axe"?

2. *Personality.* Singers with overly assertive or egocentric personalities are usually poor choices for teamwork activities such as choral performance. Conversely, luke-warm individuals whose motors seem to be constantly in idle offer little for dynamic organizations. Look for enthusiastic singers. As Joseph Huszti, Director of Choral Activities at Boston University, puts it, "Look for the intangible personality sparkle, the sparkle in the eyes."[1]

PLANNING EVENTS

Locating Potential Concerts

Nothing beats an active concert schedule for group motivation and quality performance. Every choral ensemble usually has its share of traditional or "required" concerts, such as the Sunday church service or the annual spring event. Locating additional performance outlets,

---

[1] See article by Carole Glenn, "In Quest of Answers," *The Choral Journal,* XV (February, 1975), 14-17+.

however, often takes hard work and perseverance. Here are some places to begin your search.

1. *Television and radio stations.* Local networks are especially on the lookout for choral groups at Christmas time.

2. *Community events such as commemorative ceremonies, special presentations, and annual banquets.* Check local newspapers for upcoming events.

3. *Conventions—musical and non-musical.* Contact the sponsoring organization directly. The following professional music organizations sponsor choral group performances:

- American Choral Directors Association (district and national conventions)
- American Musicological Society
- College Music Society
- Music Educators National Conference (regional and national meetings)

4. *Music and arts festivals.* These are usually advertised through brochures or newspapers.

5. *Hospitals and retirement homes.* Veteran's Administration hospitals often run a busy concert program for their patients and provide excellent performance facilities. Audiences are always appreciative.

6. *Other choral groups.* Exchange concerts and combined presentations are great avenues for sharing musical enthusiasm.

Setting up the Concert Season

Planning musical events for an entire year requires foresight and attention to detail. For example, what would happen to your school vocal group if you scheduled its last performance of the season in early April? Several important coordinating factors should be considered when you prepare long-range concert schedules.

1. *Potential conflicts.* Planning a community choral concert on the night of a local election could result in a complete flop. Note all important events which have already been scheduled and then try to work around them.

2. *Spacing.* Make sure groups of concerts and tours are spread throughout the entire year. If you are planning a cluster of concerts,

such as part of a tour, allow for sufficient "recuperation time" between performances.

3. *Variety.* Videotaping a television concert is a great experience plus hard work. More than two of these events a year become tedious.

4. *Repertoire demands.* The local businessmen's club may want your group to perform two days after the annual Christmas concert —and most of them will be there, too! Will you need new repertoire?

5. *Compatible concert situations.* Madrigals are not well received at football half-time shows. Be sure that the organization sponsoring the concert knows what kind of repertoire you perform.

The Planning Calendar

Listing the dates and times of upcoming concerts is one way to keep track of events. Calendars, however, offer a better perspective because they clearly reveal time *between* concerts. And, as we all know, directors see these intervening periods as valuable rehearsal time. Calendars with write-in space for each date work best. Here are two further suggestions which I have found to work particularly well.

1.   Align small monthly calendars side by side and paste on a cardboard backing. This will provide you with the "big picture."

2.   For weekly church planning, cut horizontal slits within each Sunday calendar square. Cut small cards which will slide halfway into these slits. Print proposed anthems on the cards and then move them around to get variety.

Computing Rehearsal Time

Assessing the total hours necessary to learn and perform repertoire for an entire program is a difficult task. Sometimes factors such as unusually high absence slow down progress, and time estimates must be continually revised. The only way to compute required rehearsal time is to have an intimate knowledge of your ensemble's capabilities and then to analyze each musical work, utilizing the following criteria:

- Length of the work
- Level of note learning difficulty
- Level of technical difficulty
- Level of interpretive difficulty

- Special coordinating problems (use of additional instruments, divided choirs, and so on)
- Memorization time (if applicable)

At this point I find it useful to plan blocks of rehearsals according to three basic phases.

- Phase I—Note Learning and Technical Mastery
- Phase II—Polishing
- Phase III—Interpreting

This approach allows the choral ensemble the opportunity to learn and develop its repertoire as a composite, organic unit. More variety is also achieved by moving from work to work within each phase. Preparing choral music in three phases is fully covered in Chapter 10.

5

How to Manage Choral Groups Efficiently and Effectively

CHOOSING FACILITIES, EQUIPMENT, AND WARDROBE

The thorough choral director is very much aware how physical factors effect the success of his ensemble. Seeking improvements is a continual process and may include such actions as immediate relocation to a better rehearsal hall or long-term budgeting for replacement choir robes.

The Rehearsal Room

People learn best under ideal conditions. A choral group able to develop proper listening and performing habits because of good rehearsal facilities can cope with inferior concert conditions if it has to. The reverse, however, will not hold true. The following factors should be considered when you are evaluating a rehearsal facility:

1. *Location of the room.* Have you ever tried rehearsing next to a buzz saw? I once had such an experience; the choral practice room was located next to the industrial arts shop. The rehearsal facility should be isolated from extraneous noises.

2. *Size of the room.* A typical classroom will not properly accommodate a sixty-voice choral ensemble. Singers need breathing room and will perform better if given adequate space. On the other hand, a facility which is too large for the group can cause a lack of intimacy—a critical ingredient necessary for effective rehearsals. This is why large, empty church sanctuaries do not always make the best rehearsal facilities.

3. *Acoustics*. Various components, such as sound dispersion, affect the acoustics of a room. But by far the most important consideration for musical performance is reverberation. Rooms which offer insufficient echo are called "dry"; those creating excessive feedback are considered to be "too live." There is no such thing as optimum reverberation time. For example, organ and wind instruments need a more lively room than a cappella voices. Even the style of music being performed creates different demands. Full-bodied Romantic period harmonies need more time to unfold than Classic era polyphony.

The best way to "get the feel" for a new rehearsal facility when it is empty is to clap your hands and sing while walking around the room. If there appears to be a moderate amount of reverberation, the room may be tentatively chosen for use. But it is only with actual performance and filled seats that you will know for sure how appropriate the facility is.

One effective method for controlling reverberation is to mount ceiling-to-floor curtains at one end of the room (opposite from the singers). These draperies may be opened or closed according to desired effect, and the material should be thick for maximum absorbency. Other more costly methods include installation of acoustical ceilings and carpeting.

4. *Seating*. If possible, movable chairs should be used rather than permanently fixed seats. They allow for temporary rearrangements of ensemble sections as well as for addition or subtraction according to actual need. Chairs should have fairly straight backs and moderate seat depth. Church pews are generally poor for rehearsing because of unusually deep seats.

5. *Lines of sight*. Often overlooked until music making actually begins are the angles of vision necessary between the director and all musicians. When pianos and organs are involved, be sure that the accompanist will have eyeball contact with you before you assign choral members to their positions. Direct lines of sight between the conductor and all singers is best facilitated by using risers or a podium.

6. *Lighting and heating*. Adequate light is obviously necessary to prevent eyestrain when choral members are reading those small notes. Proper temperature is also important. A hot room results in lethargic response; a cold room will literally put a chill on making music. Proper ventilation prevents stuffiness; however, the facility should be free from cold-producing drafts.

7. *Appearance of the room.* Singing is directly affected by the general mood of the singer, and an attractive room can do much to help promote a positive mood. Items such as posters from previous concerts, framed letters of appreciation, and helpful hints for singers can be fastened to the walls. Be sure that housekeeping standards are maintained.

I once had morale problems with a former ensemble. The "middle-of-winter doldrums" had struck, and everyone was complaining about the drab weather. This gave me an idea. Why not do everything possible to make the rehearsal room "undrab"? I asked the student officers for help and suggestions. First, we painted the room pale yellow. Then, we had some tired-out fluorescent lights replaced with new ones. Finally, we decorated the room with travel agency pictures of Hawaii. Our plan worked like a "shot in the arm." There was significant improvement in interest, vitality, and enthusiasm.

Storage Facilities

Proper storage satisfies three basic requirements:

- It protects items and supplies from abuse and pilferage.
- It helps to prevent misplacement and disorder.
- It creates more work space.

Storage necessary to accomplish these functions may range from several cabinets at one end of the rehearsal facility to separate wardrobe and supply rooms.

1. *Music storage.* Printed music should be protected from dust and mishandling yet be readily accessible when needed. Vertical folders in file cabinets work adequately for short octavo works, but there are better solutions. For example, Gamble Music Company (312 South Wabash Avenue, Chicago, Illinois 60604) and J.W. Pepper (P.O. Box 850, Valley Forge, Pennsylvania 19482) sell several types of filing boxes in various widths and depths for storing music. Office supply businesses now offer cabinets containing small compartments with side-entry doors. These allow music to be stacked flat and are especially useful for over-sized works.

In many organizations the singers' personal folders and music are stored between rehearsals. In such situations storage bins should be provided for each performer. The Wenger Corporation (Owatonna, Minnesota 55060) sells folder cabinets for this purpose. Or you can make a storage system yourself.

- Vertical panels may be spaced every three inches along a shelf. Each bin should then be assigned by name or number.
- Vertical panels may also be spaced inside transportable boxes (such as footlockers). These can be taken on tour.

2. *Wardrobe storage.* Closets work best, because they minimize dust. Metal wardrobe cabinets are also available at most business equipment stores. Wardrobes should not hang unprotected in a large room. Use dust covers or storage bags in these instances.

Instruments and Equipment

If two pianos are designated for practice or performance duties, guess which one usually ends up in the rehearsal room? As long as *both* instruments are of reputable quality and are properly maintained, there will be no problem. One thing is certain, an out-of-tune piano or organ will tend to produce faulty intonation among singers. Periodic servicing of instruments should be a top priority item for all choral organizations.

The purchase of equipment varies according to the size and type of vocal group as well as available funds. A model choral program could very well have all of the following items:

1. *Performance equipment*

- Conductor's chair or stool
- Conductor's music stand with light
- Conductor's podium
- Instrumentalists' chairs
- Metronome
- Music stands and lights
- Permanent risers with chairs
- Piano and organ benches and lights
- Record and tape playing equipment
- Touring risers

2. *Convenience items*

- Bulletin board
- Chalkboard
- Coat racks

- Clock
- Mirror
- Tables

3. *Supplies (not including obvious necessities)*

- Duplicating master sets (lined for notation)
- Music folders
- Music manuscript paper
- Music mending tape
- Music sorting file

Choosing a Wardrobe

Building or replacing a complete wardrobe for a sizeable choral ensemble is expensive. Furthermore, the chosen product will be scrutinized by hundreds of concert attenders. Therefore, some important decisions have to be made.

1. *Determining style and color.* Obviously, blazers would look out of place for an adult church choir. Choose appropriate outfits according to the group's basic purpose. On the other hand, do not overlook some of the creative garments now being offered by cap and gown companies and formal wear outlets. Here are some further points to consider.

- Does the sponsoring organization have traditional colors?
- If you are choosing gowns for church choir, should you maintain a traditional style (such as surplices and cassocks)? Are liturgical colors used in the sanctuary?
- Can you achieve a more striking effect by choosing contrasting colors (pastels work especially well for women's dresses)?
- If you are purchasing gowns, will the director and organist prefer gathered cuffs?

2. *Considering home-made wardrobes.* Commercial gowns are hard to beat for price as well as quality. For example, Collegiate Cap and Gown Company (1000 N. Market Street, Champaign, Illinois 61820) and E. R. Moore Company (7230 N. Caldwell, Niles, Illinois 60648) currently offer a number of inexpensive robes. Making men's blazers or suits is also a difficult task. Lately I have noticed a growing

trend toward leisure suits with matching shirts, purchased in bulk quantities at department stores.

Women's skirts and dresses, however, can be made at considerable savings, especially if the material is purchased wholesale directly from factory outlets. The following advice is offered:

- Choose wrinkle-free material. Wardrobes made from some of the new polyester fabrics are ideal for carrying on tours.
- Insist that seams be double stitched.

ACCOUNTABILITY AND MAINTENANCE

All organizations need to establish and maintain control over their money and property. Efficient choral groups are also concerned about such factors as attendance and wardrobe appearance. To oversee these responsibilities, some form of office work is required. The director of a small church choir may set up shop by simply keeping a folder containing purchase order forms, receipts, projected repertoire plans, and so on. Larger organizations will require more elaborate procedures. For example, my present choral program requires a complete file cabinet drawer. Some of the folder classifications are:

- Active correspondence
- Budget
- Instrumentalists
- Membership information
- Notification forms
- Past programs
- Potential concerts
- Reference correspondence
- Tour and transportation agencies

Balancing the Budget

Maintaining an accurate record of assets and deficits is one of the practical necessities required for all choral organizations. And the only way to really keep abreast of the group's financial situation is by subtracting individual expenses as they arise from allocated funds. I keep an exact account of all transactions by maintaining an itemized Record of Income and Expenses. (See Figure 5-1.) It is also a good idea to hold on to paid bills and past budgets for future reference.

RECORD OF INCOME AND EXPENSES			
BUDGETED AMOUNT:			$1,000
ITEM	DEBIT $	CREDIT $	BALANCE $
Christmas Music. Werlein's	375		625
Ticket Proceeds from Fall Concert		500	1,125
Replacement Robes	630		495
Spring Music. Werlein's	350		145

Figure 5-1

PRIORITY OF FINANCIAL NEEDS

- Printed music
- Accompaniment instruments (including maintenance and tuning)
- Performance equipment (music stands, risers)
- Wardrobe
- Concert expenses (programs)
- Travel and touring expenses
- Storage facilities
- Instrumentalist fees

NOTE: Accompanist fees and rehearsal room rental must also be included, if applicable

---

Figure 5-2

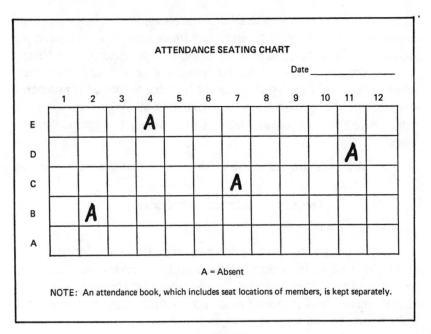

Figure 5-3

Only in rare instances does a director find himself in a position to purchase almost anything at will because of unlimited funds. Usually a priority system must be established, based on immediate versus long-range requirements. This hierarchy of financial needs will, of course, vary from one group to the next. Figure 5-2 represents one solution for organizing contemplated purchases according to priorities.

Attendance

Most choral ensembles require regular attendance, because they realize that only with commitment can musical goals and standards be reached. Therefore, some method of accounting for absences becomes necessary. In small choirs this can be accomplished by looking around and making a mental note of anyone missing. Larger groups should have singers sign in, using an attendance form. If permanent seats are assigned, the easiest method is to use an attendance seating chart. (See Figure 5-3.)

Disseminating and Accounting for Music

When new music arrives from a publisher or distributor, it should be immediately numbered and stamped with the choral organization's name. This is the only way to control the dissemination of music. Each singer is assigned a folder (preferably with storage pockets) containing his name and number, and a record of this is kept. When the new music is ready for distribution, it can be spread out on a table in numerical order. This saves time by allowing the member to locate his numbered copy before the rehearsal begins. Make sure all singers are aware of your procedures and advise them of the following suggested regulations:

- Members are responsible for loss or damage of music and folder.
- Avoid exposure to inclement weather.
- Use pencil only.

Occasionally directors from other organizations want to borrow music, or singers in your group would like to review selections not included in their current repertoire. For these purposes an index card file of music checked out to special individuals must be maintained. Information should include:

- Date music was checked out
- Title of music
- Number of copies
- Intended due date
- Signature of person checking out music

When you are storing the organization's music, alphabetical filing by composer or title rather than seasonal or functional classification works best. For example, Magnificats are usually considered to be Christmas music, but they may be performed at other times of the year. In smaller choral libraries simply placing octavo music alphabetically and doing the same with larger works will enable you to choose possible selections by scanning. Larger libraries, however, require a separate card index system. As new music is added to the organization's collection, the following information should be logged in:

- Composer's name
- Title of work
- Publisher
- Choral scoring

- Number of copies
- Performance time
- Filed location

Maintenance

Upkeep of choral organization property is another practical necessity. Unfortunately, it is a chore sometimes overlooked until a serious problem actually arises. Ideally, maintenance and housekeeping should be fully entrusted to custodial staff and hired technicians. More often, however, it requires your close attention. The piano that was "supposed to have been tuned" could turn a concert into a real disaster. Sometimes incidental duties, such as replacing a burned out music stand lamp, are best handled by the director. The following areas of concern should be periodically checked and action taken as necessary:

1. Keyboard instruments
   Besides maintaining proper intonation, check for physical abuse, cleanliness, and foreign objects inside.
2. Wardrobes
   Look for physical wear (especially frayed cuffs), spots, stains around the collar, and excessive wrinkles.
3. Music folders
   Repair tears with invisible mending tape. Replace unusable copies.
4. High fidelity equipment
   Be on the lookout for inoperative speakers, unusual hums, and faulty mechanical operation.
5. Lights and lamps
   Check for burned out bulbs, frayed wires, and loose fixtures.

RAISING MONEY

Some choral organizations are financially well off; others are not so fortunate. There are three basic reasons why most singing groups should consider raising money for themselves.

1. *To survive*. Many vocal ensembles exist independently from any sponsoring organization. For them, finding enough money to cover operating costs can become a "do or die" issue.

2. *To augment the budget.* Sometimes choirs have the money to survive but want to enhance the quality of their program by bringing in additional revenue. Maybe this extra money can be used to hire instrumentalists. Another excellent reason would be to establish a scholarship fund or donate the profits to a worthy cause.

3. *To meet the costs of special projects.* Sooner or later, unusual expenses create a sudden demand for extra money. Good examples would be replacing a worn-out wardrobe or purchasing a new piano. Choir tours and special invitations to perform in distant places create similar demands.

Sources

Several potential avenues of financial support are available. But, before pursuing these courses of action, the director of a church or school choir should be certain that he has already received maximum funding for his group. For example, I proposed a special concert for the bicentennial celebration and received additional money to cover costs involved. Sometimes an extra push can spring loose extra financial support.

Sources for additional money depend on the nature of the organization. A church choir cannot depend on alumni for support, and elementary school choruses do not usually qualify for foundation grants. Here is a list of primary sources.

1. *The members themselves.* Dues are an effective means for covering minimal costs or augmenting budgets. The annual banquet is a typical expenditure for this type of income. Watch out, however, that a sudden levy or increase in fees does not result in a loss of membership.

2. *Parents and friends.* Younger performers cannot pay for such expenses as a foreign choir tour, but their parents may support the idea if it seems promising. In adult ensembles friends of members are often sympathetic to the choral group's goals and frequently attend its concerts. Direct correspondence soliciting financial support can reap monetary rewards.

3. *Alumni.* Memories of the "good old days" are usually filled with sights, *sounds,* and events. For many graduates the alma mater choir or glee club still has symbolic significance. If you work closely with alumni officers, a solid avenue of financial support can be established. Don't overlook the possibility of borrowing money from your

alumni association. One school choral group which I directed received a three-year loan to purchase a new wardrobe. The money was repaid (interest free) in annual installments by the student activities fund.

4. *Community*. Local businesses can be a tremendous source of funds, especially if their owners know that they will receive publicity for support. Some corporations encourage their branches and divisions to spend money locally each year to further public relations. What better way than to aid your choral group!

Quality ensembles sometimes draw a following of individuals who would be more than willing to make a contribution if asked. Make an attempt to draw the community closer to the organization's values and goals by actively soliciting support.

5. *Grants*. Public and private foundations at the local, state, and national levels are often on the lookout for enterprising cultural activities worthy of their support. Usually, however, you have to find *them* and convince them of your particular choral program's value. The following hints are offered:

- Sell the program's advantages over other groups. ("My ensemble performs frequently for charitable causes.")
- Pinpoint its uniqueness. ("This vocal group specializes in early period music.")
- Provide proof of its success. ("The *Townsville Times* wrote the following rave review about our last choral performance . . . .")

Methods

Procedures for raising money may be relatively conventional like soliciting advertisements for a printed program; or they might be highly imaginative. Have you ever thought of selling fire extinguishers during Fire Prevention Week? Effective methods for funding the organization are as diversified as creativity itself.

When you are beginning a financial drive, it is a good idea to elect or appoint a campaign chairman so that all aspects of the plan will be properly administered and coordinated. If items are to be sold, these can be purchased directly from a wholesaler. Several merchandising businesses offer special plans for organizations interested in raising money for themselves. Here are just a few more examples of profit-making projects.

- Make a recording of your group and sell records for profit (great for alumni support!).
- Hold benefit concerts, with the proceeds going to a choir tour, for a charity organization, and so on. Sell tickets or take up a collection.
- Sell candy, handmade jewelry, baked goods, and so on.
- Hold an auction.
- Show movies and charge admission.
- Hold a lottery.
- Conduct a "sing in." The audience pays admission to participate in the performance of a well-known choral work.
- Wash cars, serve spaghetti dinners, paint houses.

OFFICERS—FIGUREHEADS OR CRUCIAL WORKERS?

The decision whether or not to have choral group officers often rests with the director. Some organizations, however, have well-established committees charged with the power of hiring and firing conductors. The choral leader's role will therefore depend on the nature of each situation.

- With education ensembles, the director should serve as an adviser and encourage student officers to make responsible decisions.
- With adult choral groups, he should choose the role of trouble-shooter by making recommendations for smoother, more efficient operation.

Are Officers Really Necessary?

Small church choirs seldom need officers because of the relatively straightforward operation of the music program. Sometimes a single member is given the responsibility of looking after the wardrobe. Otherwise the director handles all duties as part of his job. Professional and university choral groups often hire a business manager or secretary.

Regardless of who makes the decision to choose officers, one thing is certain: they must have a purpose. This means that responsibilities must be split between the director and the officers. In some cases conductors allow officers to participate in repertoire selection; in other instances directors prefer to reserve certain non-musical decisions for themselves. For example, I line up concert appearances and then turn the responsibility of working out the details to my officers. A very practical solution is as follows:

- The director makes all musical decisions.
- The officers carry out supportive and supplemental duties.

Officers' Individual Responsibilities

These will vary among organizations and should be tailored to fit each situation. A small group might appoint a music librarian who also handles correspondence. Figure 5-4 presents a full complement of officers and their suggested areas of responsibility for a large choral organization.

OFFICERS' RESPONSIBILITIES

President......................... overall leadership and
                                  coordination

Vice President.................. publicity, transportation,
                                  and supplies

Secretary........................ attendance, correspondence,
                                  and communication with
                                  members

Treasurer .... financial affairs

Librarian........................ music and wardrobe

Figure 5-4

Guidelines for Effectual Operation

Sometimes relationships and responsibilities between the director and the officers are allowed to deteriorate. I have known conductors who gradually assumed more and more responsibility because of undedicated officers. Here are some suggestions for maintaining a smooth administrative liason with your officers.

- Keep them informed of all decisions you have made.
- Use the chain of command. For example, do not make a decision with the treasurer without including the president in your plans.
- Allow your officers to make proper decisions and support their choices.
- Give them credit whenever it is due.
- If your officers need guidance, provide them with procedural checklists and outlines.

ORGANIZING FOR PUBLIC RELATIONS

Some school systems as well as colleges and universities have publicity or community relations offices; others do not. But one thing is certain: *you* are ultimately responsible for your choral program's public relations. An enterprising publicity office will expedite matters by opening up avenues of communication and even taking pictures. It is up to you, however, to generate news and reach out to your public.

Why Publicity?

Few choral ensembles can exist without publicity. Even the church choir, blessed with a weekly captive audience, occasionally needs to inform others about its special Sunday afternoon concert or announce a drive for new members. Public relations stimulates interest and persuades; more specifically, it can help you to do the following:

- Build the ensemble's image
- Keep students, colleagues, and administrators informed
- Let your potential audience know about upcoming concerts
- Solicit financial support
- Thank contributors

The Ingredients of Good Publicity

Many choral directors appreciate the value of publicity but are not effective in this area of responsibility. Usually, this is because they do not understand the principles behind good publicity.

1. *Message*. What are the important facts we want to communicate? Will this information help us to reach our goals?
2. *Medium*. Which channels of communication will work best for each message? How can we exploit these avenues for better publicity?
3. *Newsworthiness*. Can we tailor our messages to make them acceptable for the media? What approaches will we employ to make our facts appealing and interesting?
4. *Clarity*. How clearly do we present information? Can we "pack in" more factual data with less verbiage?
5. *Timing*. When is the most advantageous time to release our message? Do we allow for procedural lags?

Choosing Media Channels

Most people think of newspapers or radio and television when the word "publicity" is mentioned. Actually, *any* avenue which gives your group exposure, including word-of-mouth or even the concert, is a form of publicity. Here are some other channels of communication available to you.

- Telephone
- Brochures
- Mailed programs
- Posters
- Letters
- Magazines
- Records made by the ensemble

Developing a Nose for News

Newspapers are always looking for the following types of news:

1. *Spot News* consists of current information of immediate interest to readers. This week's concert or recently elected officers are good examples.
2. *Feature news* is based on human interest stories. Often this information has no immediacy and can be sent for release at any time. The lifestyle of twins, selected to be your joint accompanists, would make feature news.
3. *Photo news* usually takes the form of a picture supported by a caption or brief article. I prefer to provide publicity photographs for this purpose.

Preparing the Press Release

The press release is the proper instrument for getting information to newspapers, magazines, as well as radio and television stations.

1. *Mechanics.* The release should be typed, using double or triple spacing. Use one side of an 8½ x 11 inch piece of plain white paper. Your name, the organization, address, and telephone number should be placed in the upper left-hand corner. In the upper right-hand corner, give the date and indicate whether the story should receive immediate or delayed release. If you make a typing error, do not erase or attempt to type over it. Black it out or XXXX over it with the typewriter. Clarity is important; neatness is immaterial. Check to see that all dates and times are correct and names accurately spelled. If a name, word, or title has an unusual spelling, type the letters "CQ" in parentheses after it to verify that the spelling is correct.
2. *Content.* Anyone can write a proper press release if the necessary ingredients of who, what, where, when, why, and how are included. Avoid unnecessary verbiage and refrain from editorializing, unless you are requested to do so by the editor. This includes describing a composition as "beautiful" or designating someone as "talented." It is permissible, however, to quote the subjective statements of a critic or writer.

6

Innovative Concert Programming

REPERTOIRE SELECTION

Locating music and evaluating it for suitability takes time and effort. Several years ago I had the opportunity of hearing the Ohio State University Concert Choir perform a superb concert in Vienna, Austria. The next day I visited a local music publishing house, where I stumbled into the ensemble's director. What was he doing there? He was pouring through files of music looking at interesting repertoire for future concerts.

Obviously, choosing music should be influenced by practical considerations. A junior high school choral conductor would probably have more immediate interest in Hungarian folksongs than cantatas by Webern. It is my contention, however, that better programs can be developed when one works from depth. Knowing a wide range of choral literature, including those works you may never perform, will enable you to choose for concerts with more flexibility and taste.

Aesthetic Considerations

"Learning repertoire" is the intellectual domain of choral directing. More importantly, it leads to historical and stylistic perspective which, in turn, helps to cultivate taste. For the director this means being able to differentiate between inferior works, fads, and music of true value.

This does *not* mean that popular, modern, or non-western music will be passed by. The thing that ultimately counts in your selection is a quality called "aesthetic content." This artistic value is not necessarily to be found in a work just because it is classical. In my opinion, there are places in *Jesus Christ Superstar* which have more aesthetic content than, for example, parts of Stainer's *Crucifixion*. On the other hand, there is certainly an abundance of contemporary choral literature which attempts to provide an alternative to more traditional repertoire but which fails in the end because it really has nothing of importance to say.

Identifying artistic value in choral music is an ability which usually improves with experience. Furthermore, it is a discriminating process which can be undertaken by anyone willing to question rather than blindly accept a work's potential value. The following questions are useful when you are attempting to determine aesthetic content:

1. *Is this work composed with craftsmanship?* The relationship between the music and its text should not be an awkward one. Compositional technique, regardless of style, should be permeated by a quality of workmanship.

2. *Is this work significant?* Significance implies a sense of durable character or musical purpose as opposed to triviality. Do not overlook the fact that humorous choral works may also be significant.

3. *Is this work individualistic?* Compositions which copy other composers' ideas usually lack spontaneous immediacy; music written primarily just to be different often lacks substance. An individualistic choral work possesses both of these qualities. And because of this uniqueness, it will contrast well with other works.

Guidelines for Choosing Repertoire

When you are selecting choral music for possible performance, five general guidelines should be considered.

1. *Choose music which "possesses you."* A choral ensemble is sensitive to its conductor's likes and dislikes. If the leader feels no enthusiasm for a particular work, his vocal group may very well adopt the same attitude.

2. *Choose music which you can teach and interpret.* Many of Brahms' folksong arrangements are easy to direct, but have you considered the technical agility and interpretive insight necessary to

conduct his *Deutsches Requiem?* This does not mean that we should avoid more difficult repertoire. What is needed is a realistic estimate of our *present* capabilities and a desire to grow into more demanding conducting roles through experience.

3. *Choose reliable editions.* Be on the lookout for the following potential weaknesses in printed music:

- Improper edition of choral music. Be sure that you can discern between the composer's original markings and the editor's additions and changes.
- Poor text translations. Sometimes works of superior quality are maimed by ludicrous translations.
- Transcriptions of solo or instrumental works. Many compositions lose their original quality through this "choralizing" process.

4. *Choose challenging music.* Choral directors have an obligation to choose a variety of works which will enhance their organization's musical growth. In this sense, you have an educational mission. As a rule of thumb, most selections within a concert should be of medium difficulty for your particular group. The program can then be rounded out with one or two difficult numbers and a similar number of relatively easy works.

5. *Choose "insurance" works.* If you are unsure of your upcoming season's singers, soloists, and accompanists, select several choral pieces which are certain to "get off the ground" regardless of unforeseen limitations. More difficult compositions can be chosen later, once rehearsals get underway. These selections also serve as effective vehicles for breaking in the newly formed ensemble by allowing them to develop their relationship with music as a cohesive group. Furthermore, they begin to discover their capabilities through less taxing music.

MATCHING MUSIC WITH THE ENSEMBLE

The proper choice of music for your particular choral group is important, for it will serve as an indication of your choir's apparent capabilities. Your choice of music will also reveal several things about you as a director.

- It will show whether you are an innovator or a follower.
- It will reflect your level of musicianship.
- It will serve as a barometer of your ability to get results.

Several factors must be considered when you are matching repertoire with an ensemble.

1. *Size of the group.* Composers usually write with a specific size of group in mind. J.S. Bach, for example, did not intend his church cantatas to be performed by 150 singers. And Verdi's *Te Deum* was not composed for a chamber ensemble. Large groups are better equipped to perform more sonorous dramatic music; smaller ensembles are more effective with music of a more lyrical, personal nature. Faults also show up more in smaller groups. In these instances the director should be careful to either use better singers or avoid overly demanding works.

2. *Level of ability.* It is better to perform an easy work well than a difficult work poorly. There is a difference between singing challenging choral music and performing works which are technically over the heads of the ensemble. Even if the latter can somehow be pulled off, the inordinate amount of rehearsal time and frustration involved will not justify such choices.

Background and experience of singers should also be considered when you are deciding whether or not to perform music in a foreign language. Authentic pronunciation requires time, attention, and patience. Many concerts are marred by Americanized versions. Here is a list of languages presented in order from easy to difficult.

- Latin
- Italian
- Spanish
- German
- French

3. *Sectional characteristics.* Rarely does one find a choral ensemble with equally balanced vocal sections. Usually one section is stronger or another has range limitations. But the astute choral director can turn these inequities to advantage. If you direct a choir with unusually low bass voices, consider Russian works. If the sopranos have a limited upper range, choose music with a more moderate tessitura in

the soprano part. In instances where women significantly outnumber men, SAB arrangements may be necessary.

4. *Maturity of the voices.* Obviously, Beethoven's *Missa Solemnis* would be taxing on young singers. Care must be taken to avoid straining voices with music beyond their physical capabilities. Generally, public school aged singers should sing more lyrical music. On the other hand, Poulenc's delicate *Petites Voix* would be unfavorable for a chorus of elderly matrons. Texts should also be considered in relation to maturity. Drinking songs are more suitable for college men than for small children. As a general rule, avoid texts beyond the emotional or intellectual grasp of your singers.

5. *Available soloists.* Employing individual singers in concerts always ensures variety as well as individual motivation. Be on the lookout for works which will highlight your best soloists.

When you are matching music with the ensemble, your choices should also be tempered by the tastes of your singers. I once talked at length with a conductor who complained about his choir's disinterest in his repertoire selections. He claimed that he liked classical choral music and his singers did not. When I questioned him about his actual choices, I discovered that he tended to pick sombre sacred works. I suggested that he consider Renaissance dance songs, Baroque court music, and so on as well. The conductor was later happy to report that his singers had developed a new interest in classical choral music.

CALCULATION OF PERFORMANCE CONDITIONS

Individual concerts should not be conceived merely as isolated events. They should be planned in conjunction with the group's seasonal schedule. In New York City, where choral ensembles vie for audiences, the ability to produce contrasting programs can mean the difference between a well-attended concert and a half-empty house. Some singing organizations, including those sponsored by schools, book their performances and plan repertoire as much as three years in advance. In calculating conditions of an individual performance, the director should employ a two-stage method of planning.

General Planning

If you consider those factors which indirectly influence each concert situation, repertoire for a specific performance can be chosen with a sense of overall perspective. The most important general planning factors are:

1. *Time of season.* During the beginning of a new season, choral ensembles are still in their formative stage. Voices are not yet fully conditioned, and blend may still be shaky. Repertoire should be chosen which does not show off these potential weaknesses. On the other hand, a more aggressive program may be planned for later seasonal events.

2. *Available rehearsal time.* Demanding works require more rehearsal time. Programming for a specific concert must take this into consideration. Sometimes you may want to borrow rehearsal time before one concert to prepare for a bigger concert at a later date. This may require a more conservative choice of repertoire for the earlier program.

3. *Educational commitment.* Most school directors feel a sense of responsibility for providing a wide variety of musical experiences to their singers. Over a two- or three-year period they may complete a "repertoire cycle," which allows the graduating student to become familiar with choral music from all stylistic periods. In terms of planning this may mean presenting, for example, a festival of Renaissance music, followed by a program of Baroque and contemporary music. Or it may require incorporating selections from all stylistic periods within each concert program.

4. *Relationship with other concerts.* As was previously mentioned, contrasting concerts should be offered to returning audiences. But when *different* audiences are involved, valuable time can be saved if you choose flexible works which can be performed under a variety of concert situations. For example, compositions based on Psalm 96 ("O sing unto the Lord a new song") are appropriate for both Christmas and Easter concerts.

Specific Planning

I'll never forget the time I sang "Get Me to the Church" at a banquet only to discover later that the audience consisted of non-drinking persons of great religious zeal. To ensure success, each upcoming concert situation must be thoroughly checked, or you, too, will run the risk of running into unexpected surprises. Here are some specific planning factors to consider.

1. *Type of concert.* A Christmas candlelight service requires a completely different repertoire than a school homecoming reunion concert. The following questions should be answered for each impending concert situation:

- Does the concert under consideration have a preconceived theme?
- Will other groups or activities be involved?
- Will you use more than one ensemble?

2. *Length of concert.* If your group's presentation is being sponsored by another organization, a mutually agreeable concert length must be worked out. Radio and television studios expect very accurate control of this, and you should plan on spending several rehearsals just meeting their time requirements. Luncheon entertainments would, of course, be more flexible. Most choral concerts unhampered by time restrictions run between one and one and a half hours. The presentation of a major work, such as a Handel oratorio, could take longer.

3. *Type of audience.* Singing for a convention of Elks will be quite a different experience from performing for the women's auxiliary tea. It is always a good idea to form a generalized opinion about your audience; then plan your concert accordingly. Be especially careful about singing in foreign languages, or you will run the risk of "losing" your listeners. Unless you are performing for a sophisticated audience, plan to provide translations of foreign texts.

4. *Facilities.* Have you ever tried performing a fast-moving Baroque fugue in a resonant cathedral? Whenever possible, individual selections should be geared to concert facilities. Some things to look for include the following:

- *Acoustics.* Motets sound better in buildings with vaulted ceilings than within the confines of a television studio. Regardless of your choice, all selections should be modified in tempo by the concert hall's acoustics. (The slower the reverberation time, the slower the tempo.)
- *Staging.* Will your group perform on stage, "in the round," or in a balcony? Can you split your ensemble and perform polychoral works?
- *Accompanying instruments.* Do not expect your accompanist to play "Boogie Woogie Bugle Boy" on an organ just because

a piano is unavailable. Will the facility's keyboard instruments
be properly tuned for your performance?

- *Lighting.* Make sure all musicians, especially the instrumentalists, will be able to see you and their music properly. It may
be necessary to use music stand lamps. Don't forget the extension cords!

PROGRAM CONSTRUCTION

Many choral directors select individual works for a concert
through a process of weeding. That is, after reviewing a pile of music,
they choose several works for performance. The problem with such an
approach is that it leads to what can best be described as aimless
programming. According to Kurt Thomas, this method "reflects a
basic lack of judgment, much like the placement of paintings in a
museum without any logical order or relationship."[1]

While it is true that repertoire should suit ensemble needs and
abilities, it is also evident that selections chosen around a prearranged
theme, concept, or overall scheme will result in a better package presentation. The old expression "the sum is greater than its parts" only
holds true for programs which have been successfully designed.

Principles of Programming

Constructing a program obviously requires common sense. For
example, one should generally avoid placing a vocally demanding
choral work at the beginning of a concert. Sandwiching short, lighter
selections between heavier compositions of similar length is, likewise,
to be avoided.

Programming, like performance, is also an art. And like other arts
it is subject to certain fundamental assumptions. One of these basic
truths states that a superior work of art exemplifies the following
qualities:

- Unity
- Variety
- Coherence

Let us see how this statement can be applied to artistic programming.

---

[1]Kurt Thomas, *The Choral Conductor.* Translated by Alfred Mann and William H. Reese.
(New York: Associated Music Publishers, 1971), p. 82.

1.   *Unity.* The easiest way to achieve unity is, of course, to
perform a single major work. Many directors, however, overlook the
importance of unity when they are putting together a program of
shorter selections. Here are some solutions.

- Perform compositions by the same composer. This approach
  allows for an acquaintance in depth with one composer's output.
- Perform works from the same genre. I once performed a very
  successful "Festival of Magnificats." It is often quite interesting to hear how various composers have treated a specific type
  of composition.
- Perform choral cycles. These include not only groups of songs
  by one composer but also cycles made up by the director from
  isolated compositions. For example, the theme "Songs of Nature" can provide a thread of continuity between selections.
  This approach also helps to sustain interest in an entire group
  of choral works.

2.   *Variety.* One argument against unity is that such programs
can become boring ("Who wants to listen to a whole evening of
Renaissance motets?"). Planned variety, however, will guarantee
against boredom in properly constructed programs. Some basic ways
to obtain variety are as follows:

- *Changes in mood.* The mood of a particular work is influenced
  by such elements as tempo, mode, dynamic level, harmonic
  treatment, and text.
- *Changes in ensembles, soloists, and accompanying forces.*
  One way to capture an audience's attention is by opening a
  program with a Gregorian chant sung by the men followed by a
  polyphonic version of the same chant performed by the entire
  mixed choir.
- *Groups of sacred compositions interspersed with groups of
  secular works*
- *Juxtaposition of early period with late period selections.* For a
  delightful effect, try a back-to-back presentation of *Hodie
  Christus Natus Est* by Poulenc (a cappella), Monteverdi
  (women's voices), and Sweelinck (with organ and cello).
- *Long works interspersed with groups of short compositions*

3. *Coherence*. This quality applies to the sense of continuity or cohesion within an entire program. A presentation may gain unity through the choice of a theme, but it will become coherent only as a result of overall design. Some types of programs which achieve coherence in varying degrees include the following:

- *Chronological*. The most popular approach.
- *Heavy to light*. Works best with audiences of limited attention span.
- *Featured work*. Key composition chosen first; other repertoire selected to complement major work.

One of the best and most imaginative ways to achieve coherence is by incorporating unified groups of songs, contrasting ensembles, and so on into an overall scheme which I call "framing."

- Choose beginning and ending compositions first. The opener might be an effective show piece; the closing number could have brightness or humor.
- Next, choose works which will bracket the intermission. These should have impact yet not overshadow the beginning and ending selections.
- Finally, choose contrasting groups of works, ensembles, "mood pieces," and so on which effectively complement the compositions already selected.

Framing is a useful approach for obtaining program balance as well as coherence.

DESIGNING AND SUPERVISING THE PRINTED PROGRAM

The printed program is intended to provide attractively essential information about your concert's repertoire and its participants. Just how much information is necessary will depend on the formality of the concert. A short mid-day presentation would probably require only a brief listing of works to be performed, and the director might verbally announce supplementary information such as the names of soloists. On the other hand, a formal concert would require a full printed program, which might include all of the following information:

1. *Program cover or heading.* (See Figure 6-1.) As with good newspaper reporting, several basic questions must be immediately answered for the program reader.

- Who? What performing group is involved? If several ensembles will perform, they may be listed separately or given a collective name such as "The Edison High School Choral Groups." Include the names of the director and accompanists. Soloists may also be listed here or within the context of the program repertoire.

- What? Describe the type of concert, whether it is simply "A Choral Concert" or a more specific type such as "The Third Annual Christmas Choral Pageant."

- Where? Even though the audience obviously knows where it is, the concert location should be provided. Programs are often filed for reference or passed on to others, and this information becomes necessary.

- When? Give the date, including the year, and the time of the concert.

2. *The repertoire to be performed.* (See Figure 6-2.) Usually prefaced by the heading "Program," this part of your printed program must be carefully laid out so that your audience does not get lost. Care must be taken to set off groups of selections from one another by using double spacing. The names of ensembles should be printed with bold-face type or capital letters. Soloists' names must be placed closely with the title of the work in which they will perform. Here are some further suggestions regarding program entries.

- When listing composers' names, be specific. Did you know that two members of the illustrious Bach family composed Magnificats? Be sure that you include first initials when you are dealing with composers with identical last names. Better yet, print full names and avoid such potential problems.

- List the complete title of program entries. "Kyrie Eleison" by Schubert does not give the listener sufficient information since we know that the composer wrote "Kyries" for six different Latin Masses. If the selection is taken from a larger work, let people know.

ANNUAL SPRING CONCERT

performed by

Philomusica

LEWIS GORDON, Director
LILIAN KESSIN, Accompanist

Saturday, April 29, 1972
New Brunswick High School
New Brunswick, New Jersey
8:30 p.m.

Sunday, May 7, 1972
Trinity Presbyterian Church
East Brunswick, New Jersey
4:00 p.m.

Saturday, May 13, 1972
Kirkpatrick Chapel
Rutgers University
New Brunswick, New Jersey
8:30 p.m.

Figure 6-1

PROGRAM

THE UNIVERSITY SINGERS —

Magnificat .Giovanni Battista Pergolesi
    1. Magnificat anima mea
    2. Et misericordia: Fecit potentiam
        Cheryl Roberts, soprano; Vicki Mitchell, alto
    3. Deposuit potentes
    4. Suscepit Israel
        Ray Williams, tenor; John Odom, bass
    5. Sicut locutus est
    6. Sicut erat in principio
    Assisted by the String Ensemble

Locus iste a Deo factus est . . . . Anton Bruckner

Alleluia . . . . .Randall Thompson

THE USM CHAMBER SINGERS —

Three Sixteenth-Century Spanish Carols . . . . Anonymous
    1. E la don don, verges María
        Lonnie Nielsen, tenor
    2. Dadme albricias, hijos d'Eva
        Sharon Penley, soprano; Michael Carter, tenor
    3. Ríu, ríu, chíu
        Randy Cuchens, bass

O magnum mysterium . . . . Tomas Luis de Victoria

Magnificat . . . . Johann Pachelbel

THE COMBINED CHORAL GROUPS —

A Hymn to the Virgin . . . . Benjamin Britten

Christmas Cantata . . . . Daniel Pinkham
    1. Quem vidistis pastores?
    2. O magnum mysterium
    3. Gloria in excelsis Deo
    Assisted by the Brass Ensemble

Figure 6-2

- Differentiate between composers and arrangers. *Shenandoah* was not composed by Gregg Smith; it was arranged by him (as well as others). Use the abbreviation "Arr." before arrangers' names.

3. *Supplementary information*. The following items should be considered for each printed program:

- Translations. It is usually helpful to provide listeners with translations of foreign texts performed in the concert. Very short translations can be included within the program of repertoire. More lengthy translations should be placed on another page of the printed program or disseminated separately.

- Program notes. These may include background information about musical selections or biographical data about individual performers. Newsworthy items about the ensemble or upcoming auditions are also worth listing.

- Participating musicians. Keep in mind that concerts are performed by people who appreciate seeing their names on a program, especially if the event has personal significance for them. The concert goer may not know 95 percent of the performers, but you can be sure that he will be looking on the printed program for the names of those he does know.

- Sponsors. Individuals or businesses who have contributed financially toward the choral organization deserve mention in your program.

- Acknowledgments. Quite often others are partly responsible for.your concert's success. These individuals may range from the orchestra director who helped to prepare the instrumental accompaniment to students who sold tickets for the presentation. While a handshake or a letter of appreciation is always welcomed, the best way to show your appreciation is by noting these people and their contributions in your printed program.

Program Appeal

The printed program does far more than provide essential information; it also *conditions* the audience for the concert. The expectant mood created within the listener will often be dependent on the printed program's appearance as well as its content. For example, if you attended a formal evening concert, how would your attitude be affected by a poorly-spaced, half-faded, slightly angled program duplicated on a "ditto" machine?

Needless to say, printed programs can be expensive for a small ensemble operating on a shoestring budget. Sometimes, however, imagination and attention to detail can offset financial limitations. Here are some things to consider.

1. *Physical layout.* The number of pages in a program is, for the most part, controlled by the amount of information to be printed. The size and design of those pages, however, is open to far more ingenious ideas than the standard rectangular format.

- Experiment with unusually wide or long pages. Printers can reduce letter size to comfortably fit an entire program of repertoire on a 6 x 12 inch sheet of paper.

- Consider programs with rounded corners or frayed edges.

- Have programs folded accordion style into several pages.

2. *Color and texture.* A visit to the printer's shop will reward you with a surprising discovery of what is really available for printed programs.

- Consider the wide latitude of light-colored and textured paper now available.

- Choose different colors for printing. Dark-red ink on light-beige paper is very effective.

- Have the program run off on several different pastel-colored packs of paper. Then, shuffle these various-colored programs before distributing them to the audience. This approach is especially effective for festivals and lighter concerts.

3. *Print.* Most programs are too conservative in their use of print to set off titles, names of ensembles, and so on.

- Request printers to use lettering of various heights and thicknesses.

- Choose print which matches the type of program you will be presenting. Old English lettering goes well with Renaissance programs; sleek print looks good for contemporary programs.

Supervising the Printing of the Program

Many choral concerts have been blemished by printed programs which omitted information or contained misspelled names. I once approved for printing a beautiful program which failed to mention the name of the performing group! Care must be especially taken when you are dealing with peoples' names. Is your accompanist's first name Marianne, Maryanne, or Mary Ann?

Directors sometimes make a false assumption that scribbling out a program for the secretary to type is sufficient. The only way to ensure the printed program's success is through follow-up action. Even when an officer or choral secretary has been given responsibility for this project, *you* are accountable for the finished product. The following steps will help to guarantee the program's success:

- Start by typing a rough draft to determine spacing and overall layout.
- Type a final draft and proofread it before sending it to the printer.
- Request galley proofs from the printer and proofread these before approving the actual printing.

Proofreaders sometimes fall into the trap of reading programs for content rather than accuracy. For this reason it is a good idea to have a second proofreader.

When you are ordering programs, be sure that you request enough for an unexpected bumper crop of listeners. People will share if they have to, but running out of programs is like inviting guests for dinner and not having enough food. Finally, provide typists and printers with sufficient time to meet your concert deadlines comfortably. When you are using professional printers, plan to have weekend concert programs delivered the Thursday before the presentation. This allows an extra day for delivery vehicle breakdown, unexpected snowstorms, and so on.

7

Developing Stylistic Accuracy
in Choral Performance

American choral groups are highly regarded for their polished sound and enthusiastic sonorities. I must confess, I have found little in life which can equal the excitement of a thundering chorus performing Berlioz's *Te Deum*. Unfortunately, some directors attempt to interpret a Bach cantata or even a Morley madrigal the same way.

I have had discussions with choral directors who voiced concern that changing vocal interpretation for different stylistic periods would ruin their ensembles' blend and tone quality. This attitude, however, is ill-founded, because it presumes that each choral group should have a preconceived sound. Every quality choir I have ever heard had *control*, which is completely different from the "one-sound approach." And, more important, each was able to adapt to the music's stylistic demands rather than subjecting a large portion of choral repertoire to the meat-grinder treatment.

This discussion about stylistic interpretation can best be clarified by answering three essential questions.

1. *Why attempt to achieve stylistic accuracy?* The most obvious answer is: to avoid boredom. When I read music critics' reviews of choral concerts, one frequent criticism I find are statements to the effect that everything sounded the same. Choral performances are sometimes bland not simply because of poor programming but because of insufficient stylistic interpretation.

There is, however, another, more important reason for performing repertoire with stylistic distinction: music only comes to life when its essence is revealed. You may somehow "pull off" a performance with technical proficiency and impressive talent, but you will only bring a work to life by fulfilling its stylistic requirements.

2. *What are the problems encountered when you are attempting to achieve stylistic accuracy?* Most difficulties of choral music before the Romantic period are related to its accompaniment. Few ensembles have ready access to authentic instruments used in early period performances. This usually means that a compromise must be made by employing modern instruments and encouraging methods of playing which will bring out as much as possible of the music's early flavor. For example, string players must be shown how to bow and embellish Baroque works.

On the other hand, harpsichords and recorders are sometimes available, and a little extra effort by the director to locate and use these instruments will go far toward providing a more realistic performance. Not to be overlooked are commonly available percussion instruments which are similar in sound to those used in Renaissance presentations. It is surprising how much vitality can be brought to the interpretation of a sprightly Spanish villancico by simply adding a tambourine or snareless drum.

Recently I had the opportunity to hear two contrasting interpretations of Giovanni Gabrieli's polychoral motet *Jubilate Deo*. The first presentation employed organ accompaniment with the double choir. The second performance, however, doubled the voices with two choirs of brass instruments and used the organ accompaniment more judiciously to reinforce climactic sections. This interpretation was an exhilarating one, and primarily because the motet received proper stylistic attention.

3. *How can stylistic accuracy best be achieved?* Correct interpretation begins with the director's concept of style. This means that you must learn to recognize styles not only by but also within each period. For instance, Vaughan-Williams and Ligeti are twentieth century choral composers; yet the stylistic requirements of their music differ sharply. Often differences between national styles and even genres must be taken into account.

After the director knows what he wants, methods must be found to communicate this information to the performers. Singers need to hear a demonstration of Renaissance vocal tone. Through trial and error various concepts and descriptive ideas are conveyed until the ensemble begins to work successfully toward desired interpretation.

Often one word may have an impact on the group and become a trigger for correct stylistic response. I once had difficulty with my choir's interpretation of a Bach cantata until I described the fugue they were performing as "sewing machine music" and asked them to "chatter" as they sang. My imagery hit home, and their interpretation snapped into focus.

Some directors prefer to deal exclusively with technical instructions when they are working with singers. This will not always work when you are trying to achieve stylistic accuracy. For example, you may rightly ask for minimal vibrato in a Gesualdo chromatic madrigal, but it will be the ensemble's *concept* of overall mood and tonal quality which will determine the final interpretative outcome of the work.

MUSIC TO 1600

The Medieval and Renaissance eras represent an extensive period of at least eleven hundred years. In spite of various stylistic trends, however, there are several musical characteristics which permeate most music from this early period.

- Melodic and linear movement of lines takes precedence over harmonic considerations.
- Modality, rather than tonality, provides characteristic color of all genres until at least 1500.
- Rhythm is often non-metrical and unstressed.

This extensive period also includes a notable achievement in music history. Gregorian chant and other single line vocal music gave ground to the composition of sacred and secular multi-part works. Because of different stylistic demands, each category is presented separately.

Gregorian Chant

Also known as plainsong, this monophonic vocal music was originally conceived for musical enhancement of the early Christian Church Offices and Masses. Chant is restrained and relatively unemotional so as not to interfere with the dignified nature of these services. Melodic movement is primarily step-wise; disjunctive skips and leaps are conservative. Rhythm is free flowing and largely determined by the text and its treatment. For example, Alleluias are melismatic (many notes to one syllable), whereas the many-worded Glorias and Credos are predominantly syllabic (one note per syllable).

1. *Performers.* Gregorian chant is unison music primarily for men's voices. Convents, however, were established as early as the fifth century where nuns participated fully in chanting. During the Renaissance period male choirs, consisting of boys and men, performed this vocal music in octaves. My personal preference is to use either males *or* females for Gregorian chant performances. This practice tends to convey a more appealing, authentic interpretation to present-day concert audiences.

Organs were installed in churches as early as the Middle Ages, but they were probably used more for the accompaniment of congregational hymns than for chants. The size of the choir varied from a half dozen singers in a small country church to a large contingent of monks at a monastery. Generally speaking, chanting is best performed by a small to moderate sized choral group.

The director should not fall into the trap of performing all chants with full forces. Psalms require responsorial treatment. This means that a soloist should alternate with the ensemble. Certain sections of the Mass, such as the Introit, Offertory, and Communion, require alternation between two choirs, called "antiphonal style." Modern chant books and choral editions often provide directions in this regard. Catholic clergy are usually willing to provide additional help.

2. *Stylistic requirements.* Chanting still exists as an integral activity of the Catholic Church service. But in many instances its practice has been modernized by English translation, organ accompaniment, and so on. When chant is sung in Latin, local and regional versions of pronunciation often prevail. The director should choose a widely accepted pronunciation guide and require his singers to follow its rules. I prefer *Pronunciation of Church Latin,* a brochure printed by the American Guild of Organists (630 Fifth Avenue, New York, New York 10020).

- *Tonal color.* Purity of tone with little or no vibrato was the objective sought by early singers. This essential character of chant will be attained as your singers learn to hit each pitch "dead center" without slurring. An emphasis on vowels, and a slight de-emphasis on such aspirated consonants as "t" and "k," will also help to preserve chant's legato nature. A cappella unison singing is difficult and requires special attention to intonation. One faulty voice may pull the entire ensemble off pitch. Proper blending is also important, for vocalists who stick out will tend to destroy rhythmic coordination.

- *Phrasing.* Singers must be trained to spin out phrases without taking obtrusive breaths in the middle of lines. When phrases of extended length are encountered, carefully rehearsed staggered breathing may be necessary. Chanting several syllables or words to individual tones also requires special coordination. These types of chants are frequently encountered in Renaissance Magnificats where Gregorian chant verses are interspersed with multi-part choral sections. In some instances, choosing a soloist for the chant sections may save considerable rehearsal time.

- *Dynamics.* Crescendos and decrescendos should be scrupulously avoided. Such practice was branded "self display" and condemned by church clergy. Be especially careful not to place a diminuendo on final notes.

- *Tempo.* The overall speed of a particular chant should be determined by its text. Solemn words require slower tempos; psalms of praise are more vigorous. Early period singers became adept at slowing the ends of phrases, and the director should attempt to capture this "ebb and flow," which is so essential to chanting.

3. *Improvisation.* Chants are constructed out of various modes which usually avoid leading tones. Early period singers, however, added sharps to certain notes so as to create a feeling of finality at cadences (other tones were flattened to avoid the tritone). This practice was called *musica ficta.* The problem with such alteration is that it tends to destroy Gregorian chant's modal character. For this reason I feel that *musica ficta* should be avoided when you are performing plainsong.

4. *Conducting problems.* The early practice of conducting chant with the use of suggestive pitch signs was called "chironomy." Because plainsong is based on free-verse rhythm, today's metrical patterns for conducting are really not geared to such music. Once a par-

ticular Gregorian chant has been chosen for performance, experiment with various circular and linear arm movements until motions are found which best express the character of each musical phrase.

Sacred Polyphonic Music

Early sacred multi-part music owes much of its character to pre-established Gregorian chant. It, too, is restrained and austere when compared with secular music of the same period. More importantly, plainsong is usually employed as a foundation (called a cantus firmus) within these religious works, where it quite often appears in the tenor vocal line.

The original chant is frequently separated into shorter parts by the composer so that each segment may be used to establish a different musical section. These sections are, in turn, overlapped, resulting in a continuous outpouring of sound permeated by interwoven strands of lines. Occasional contrasts are obtained through the use of less active homophonic (chordal) sections. Motets, Masses, and Magnificats comprise the bulk of early sacred polyphonic repertoire.

1. *Performers.* Church choirs varied in size from half a dozen to approximately eighteen singers. The Sistine Chapel in Rome maintained an unusually large choir of thirty performers during the Renaissance period. Obviously, presenting this type of music with a chorus of one hundred singers would be unacceptable.

Contrary to popular belief, a cappella singing was but one of several ways to perform an early sacred composition. Sometimes the church's organ was used to softly accompany the singers. Instruments, such as the fiedel (early stringed instrument), the recorder, and the crumhorn (early oboe), often doubled the vocal lines in performance.

Choral directors should experiment with combinations of available instruments and voices. Figure 7-1 presents a typical solution for achieving a more authentic sound. By employing various modes of performance, you can achieve significant contrasts. This is especially important when you are presenting several Medieval or Renaissance works within the same program.

2. *Stylistic requirements*

- *Tonal color.* As with Gregorian chant, vibrato was minimal or nonexistent. Because of closely interwoven lines, clarity of each part is essential. For this reason, vocal sections must be

---

**DISTRIBUTION OF INSTRUMENTS FOR
EARLY PERIOD SACRED MUSIC PERFORMANCE**

Vocal Part	*Doubling Instrument*
Soprano	Recorder (Flute)
Alto......................	Viola
Tenor....................	Oboe
Bass	Violoncello

Figure 7-1

encouraged to preserve the character of their particular line by blending only as a section. Balance, not blend, is important *between* vocal sections. A lighter, relatively thin tone quality is also desirable. Tenors should rely more on falsetto for high notes, and basses should make frequent use of head voice.

- *Phrasing.* Because choristers sang from part books, they became adept at observing melodic direction, spinning out phrases, and stressing important words. Contemporary directors need to spend time training their singers to think horizontally rather than vertically. The Bach chorale approach will not work for most Renaissance sacred polyphony.

- *Dynamics.* Although directions for loudness and softness were not written in the part books, dynamics were undoubtedly used in conjunction with the rise and fall of melodic lines. Certainly, textual acclamations such as "Et resurrexit . . ." called for more of a forte sound than "Et incarnatus est. . . ." Early period sacred music, however, is reserved music, and choral directors should be both conservative and discrete in their employment of dynamics.

- *Tempo.* Renaissance music was universally regulated by a relatively fixed duration of time called the "tactus" (beat). According to scholars, this uniform speed was closely related to pulse rate and is comparable to our present day slow or moderately slow tempo. Composers achieved changes in speed by changing notational values within the composition. Thus, the conductor's duty was to establish and maintain a uniform beat, allowing the music to unfold with its built-in changes of pace naturally taking place. There was, however, a tendency to gather forces together on the penultimate (next-to-the-last) tone before settling on the final note.

3. *Improvisation.* Although *musica ficta* was employed by singers, the question of when and how often to alter notes has been a perplexing one for musicologists. Introducing leading tones will make cadences more forceful, but it will also orient modal compositions more towards major or minor tonality. Modern reliable editions of Medieval and Renaissance choral music identify places where the rules of *musica ficta* may be applied by placing a sharp or flat above the pertinent note. Ultimately, however, you as the director must decide. Play through a composition using both approaches. You may choose either the plain or the altered version. When you are combining the two, be careful not to introduce inconsistencies between vocal lines.

4. *Conducting problems.* Although modern editions usually employ bar lines, downbeat stress must be minimized. One of the conductor's prime responsibilities is to maintain a steady, unaccented tempo. As a matter of fact, it would be better to establish an even series of hand or finger movements rather than forcing the ensemble to contend with an erratic conducting pattern. The left hand is especially useful for helping present-day singers with their melodic interpretation by molding and shaping individual lines at strategic places.

Secular Polyphonic Music

Early period secular choral repertoire tends to fall into two categories.

- Classic madrigals, similar in format to the religious motets. These are stylistically mannered and often depend on chromaticism for word painting and coloristic effects. Even when they are plaintive, they are more passionate than their sacred counterpart.

- Lighter Italian canzonettas, English ballads, Spanish villancicos, and so on. These are strophic works, often containing homophonic refrains in triple meter. Many are written with conciseness and tend toward a hearty, robust character.

1. *Performers*. Secular vocal music was primarily intended for private performance by small groups. Even when it was performed for the public, only one or two singers normally sang each part. The intimate nature of these works should be preserved by presenting them with chamber-sized ensembles. Many pieces are ideal for solo groups such as trios and quartets.

As with sacred choral music of the same period, instruments often doubled the vocal parts. Another prevalent practice was the substitution of instruments for voices. For example, if a bass singer was unavailable for a music-making session, a lira da gamba (early violoncello) might have been played instead. Quite often a vocal work was performed as a solo by having the top line sung while several instruments performed the bottom parts. Many late sixteenth century English ayres were provided in two versions by the composer. One arrangement required a vocal soloist accompanied by lute; the other version employed only singers.

2. *Stylistic requirements*.

- *Tonal color*. Pureness of tone and clarity of line are essential as with all early period vocal forms. More variety of color is necessary, however, than for sacred music. Composers such as Jannequin even require imitations of birds, street cries, and so on. Basses need to be nimble so that they may keep up with others in their handling of thematic material.

- *Phrasing*. Contrapuntal sections usually consist of overlapping phrases. These require catch breaths and staggered breathing so as not to interrupt momentum. Homophonic sections require coordinated ensemble breathing.

- *Dynamics*. Secular works sometimes contain repeated sections which should be performed at contrasting dynamic levels. The first statement is often sung forte; the repeat is performed piano. This process may be reversed at the end of a work to gain a more climactic effect. As with early sacred music, dynamics may be conservatively employed in conjunction with the natural rise and fall of phrases. Slight crescendos on long-held notes, especially suspensions, can be effective when they are carefully controlled.

- *Tempo.* Be on the alert for modern editions containing an overabundance of half and whole notes. Unless the work is a lamentation or a melancholic love song, this probably means that the scholar who transcribed the music from its original manuscript failed to bring his notation into line with present-day practice. Let the textual content and the overall mood of the music be a guide to your choice of tempo.

3. *Improvisation.* Besides employing the rules of *musica ficta,* singers were adept at bringing out pertinent words for dramatic effect. One should keep in mind that love songs were often composed and performed with feigned emotion. Words such as "swooning," "weeping," and "dying" should be slightly exaggerated. Dissonant, chromatically altered notes may also be leaned on to achieve their full effect.

4. *Conducting problems.* The relationship between duple and triple meter is important in early period secular music since it occurs so often within many compositions. The correct way to control these transitions is by treating the half note as a common denominator. (See Figure 7-2.)

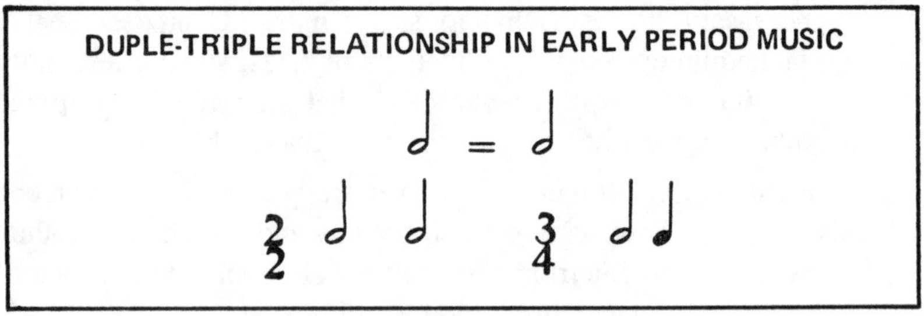

DUPLE-TRIPLE RELATIONSHIP IN EARLY PERIOD MUSIC

Figure 7-2

THE BAROQUE ERA

Unlike those of the previous period, most genres of the Baroque era were performed with similar stylistic treatment. The primary exceptions were sacred motets occasionally written and performed in the older Renaissance fashion. But, for the most part, Baroque music, whether it was courtly or religious, was greatly unified in style by the harmonically conceived basso continuo.

Melodic lines became polarized from other parts and took on a more diversified independence ranging from declamatory recitatives to lyrical arias. Modality gave way completely to tonality, and such compositional devices as modulation and functional harmony came into practice. As the period moved into maturity, two basic modes of choral treatment became prevalent and were often used interchangeably within compositions:

- Contrapuntal sections and movements, usually employing extensive runs and perpetual motion
- Homophonic sections and movements. The chorale exemplifies this type of writing.

1. *Performers.* Large performing groups were the exception rather than the rule. Many of J.S. Bach's cantatas were performed by approximately twelve singers and twenty instrumentalists. Vocal soloists came from within the choir. Instruments commonly used were recorders, viols (early stringed instruments), oboi d'amore (early oboes pitched a minor third lower), bassoons, clarin trumpets, and timpani.

A few of today's adventurous ensembles, such as university *collegium musicums,* are able to present performances using some of these authentic instruments. Directors should at least make an attempt to locate recorder players. Trumpet players who specialize in performing high notes on a modern "Bach trumpet" are sometimes available. Finding viol players is more difficult. One solution is to use gut on regular string instruments to achieve a more mellow and less penetrating sound similar to that of the earlier viols.

Instruments were often substituted for one another, depending on which players were available for performance. You should feel free to use recorders (or flutes) in place of strings and vice versa. Often a practical solution is to combine them on a particular part.

The most important thing to remember in this discussion is the fact that very little a cappella singing actually occurred. Instruments doubled vocal parts in choral works unless they had their own accompanying material to perform. Modern editions of Baroque choral music often overlook this point and fail to provide necessary instrumental parts for so-called a cappella movements. This means, for example, that J.S. Bach's motets should be performed with instruments, and their parts are to be derived from the vocal lines.

The harpsichord was the basic keyboard instrument for secular music; the organ was played in sacred performances. Reversing this procedure, or combining both instruments within the same work, was highly unusual and should be avoided. The keyboard played at all times within a composition, unless a particular section was marked "tacet" by the composer. To help solidify harmonic support, at least one bass instrument always played along with the keyboard. Violoncellos, double basses, and bassoons should be used for this function in present-day performances.

2. *Stylistic requirements.*

- *Tonal color.* Vocal agility was necessary to perform rapid florid runs. Even in slower-moving passages, thick, vibrato-ridden singing was avoided. Therefore, tone quality should be clear and relatively thin. Under no circumstances should Baroque choral music be performed using modern-day operatic force.

- *Phrasing.* Because so much of this period's music employs the principle of perpetual motion, phrases are often extensive and closely juxtaposed with minimal time for pause in between. Maintaining momentum has top priority in these situations, and choristers must learn to skillfully employ catch breaths and staggered breathing.

- *Dynamics.* Common practice was to employ either forte or piano volume and reserve other levels of dynamics for special effects. Hence, the term "terraced dynamics" has become a popular term for describing Baroque dynamics. Repetitions of phrases, especially at the end of sections and movements, were frequently performed as echoes. Dissonances were intended as expressive devices and should be performed louder than surrounding musical material.

- *Tempo.* Although much of this period's music is fast moving, tempos were always controlled and never rushed. Baroque music is metrical, and the feeling of bar line stress and rhythmic pulsation should be allowed to permeate performance.

3. *Improvisation.* Music of this period literally glittered with ornaments added to music in performance. Choral ensembles, however, were expected to perform their parts with minimal embellishment so as not to cloud their parts excessively. As a general rule, restrict choristers to trills at suitable cadences and only when they are singing the melodic line.

Vocal soloists, however, were a different matter. They were expected to ornament their music, especially when performing the repeat sections of da capo (ABA) arias. Nowadays the extent of embellishing will depend on the vocal agility of the singer chosen for performance. Coloratura sopranos are obviously capable of performing more of these flourishes than deep basses. Instrumental ensembles likewise should be encouraged and guided in their performance of ornamentation. This is especially true for instrumentalists who perform solo melodies and obbligatos.

Knowing how and when to embellish Baroque music is not always an easy task. Some choral scores designate basic locations with appropriate signs; others are remiss in this aspect. One initial aid is to listen to recordings of authentic choral performances by such groups as Nikolaus Harnoncourt's Concentus Musicus (Telefunken label), observing places in the score where embellishments occur. Consult Thurston Dart's *The Interpretation of Music* for details regarding types of ornaments and their signs.

Baroque music was also performed with stylized crispness. Dotted rhythms were normally executed as though they were double-dotted unless they occurred in conjunction with triplets. (See Figure 7-3.) If you decide to use a relatively large choral ensemble, extra time must be devoted to cleaning up rhythmic articulation as well as attacks and releases.

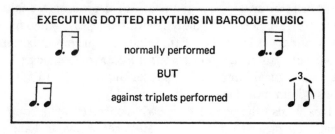

Figure 7-3

4. *Instrumental considerations.* As was previously mentioned, Baroque choral music was rarely unaccompanied. And because present-day performances are most effective when they include instrumental ensembles, a few suggestions for working with players are offered.

Strings should usually bow detaché (short, separate strokes played smoothly). Bow pressure should also be kept minimal, and vibrato and glissandos avoided. Whenever possible, metrical accents, such as the first note of a measure, should receive a down bow. Wind instruments are best played with relatively light pressure and gentle embouchure.

Contrasts are effectively achieved through careful distribution of instruments. For example, when you are performing J. S. Bach's double motets, strings should be double one choir, winds the other. Incidentally, the bass line instrument playing with the keyboard should complement other accompanying instruments whenever possible. For example, if strings are designated to perform without winds, use violoncello and possibly double bass with the keyboard; if winds play alone, use bassoon on the continuo part. When strings and winds play together, bass line instruments may also be mixed.

Occasionally a director is fortunate enough to find a viola da gamba (early violoncello) or even a complete consort of viols for performance. These instruments take longer to "speak" than modern strings and must be treated accordingly.

THE CLASSIC PERIOD

One of the outstanding characteristics of Classic period music in general is its emphasis on melodic lyricism. As a result, many melodies achieve a refined and pleasantly ingratiating quality. Harmony, often confined to an accompanistic role, is usually controlled by cleanness of progression and stylistic discreteness. Although contrapuntal writing was carried over from the Baroque era, it became more harmonically saturated. Another salient feature of Classic period music is the symmetrical structure of phrases and the clean delineation of sections within movements.

This is also the age of the newly conceived symphony, and its idiomatic characteristics permeate all other forms including choral music. For example, much of the choral writing in F. J. Haydn's

Masses is absorbed into a pervasive symphonic texture. Composers of this period were also affected by the *Sturm und Drang* (Storm and Stress) literary movement. As a result, some choral works contain an abundance of dramatic tension, particularly in developmental and climactic sections. Compositional devices used to achieve this effect include unexpected dynamic changes from piano to forte and sudden crescendos or sforzatos. Yet this display of musical force is inevitably controlled by Classic period unity and form.

1. *Performers.* Performing groups were moderate in size compared to today's standards. Even the very large Salzburg Cathedral, which was musically better equipped than most institutions, limited its performers to the following numbers:

- 8 to 10 vocal soloists
- 40 to 45 choral singers
- 25 to 30 instrumentalists

During the Classic period, the harpsichord was gradually replaced by the piano over a twenty-year period beginning about 1770. As a general rule, secular choral works composed after 1790 should use piano when keyboard accompaniment is required. Organ was, of course, still used as the accompanying keyboard instrument for sacred music.

2. *Stylistic requirements.*

- *Tonal color.* Lightness and clarity of tone are essential for achieving Classic period elegance of style. Therefore, vibrato should be minimized and lyrical buoyancy maximized in vocal production. Directors, however, should not confuse this with timidity, for a degree of assertiveness is necessary to maintain the rhythmic vitality usually found in this music.

- *Phrasing.* Musical phrases are often two or four measures in length and paired. Whenever symmetrical structure occurs, performers may be encouraged to perform a slight decrescendo at mid-cadence, followed by light stress at final cadence. This practice promotes a more distinct articulation of phrasal structure, in keeping with the style of the period.

- *Dynamics.* For the first time in music history, crescendos and decrescendos were actively employed by composers. Singers should not become too emotionally involved when they are performing these changes in loudness in order to preserve a controlled, objective mood. As with Baroque music, dissonances need emphasis.

- *Tempo*. Sensitivity to precise tempo is very important. When it is rushed, Classic period music tends to lose its stately character; when it is performed too slowly, its characteristic crispness and rhythmic vitality are lost. Pulsation is more gentle than that found in Baroque music and should not be "driven" excessively.

3. *Improvisation*. Ornamentation was still performed, but more moderately than in the former period. Trills do occur frequently but are treated differently than the "prepared trills" of the Baroque period. (See Figure 7-4.) When you are using piano for accompaniment, embellishments should be performed less frequently than for harpsichord.

Figure 7-4

ROMANTICISM

In contrast to the relatively objective and formal nature of Classic period music, Romantic era works are generally more subjective and mood conscious. Unhampered by preconceived musical forms, the Romanticists concentrated more on pure sound by striving for unusual textures and sonorities. Dissonances were employed more frequently; extensive chromaticism and remote modulations began to push tonality toward its limit.

Lyricism continued to play an important role, as evidenced by the works of Schubert and others. Melody, however, also became more subservient to harmony, even losing its identity at times as it became engulfed within harmonically conceived dramatic action. Rhythm took on a more impetuous nature through frequent employment of syncopation, surges in tempo, and sudden accents.

1. *Performers.* Most of the Romantic period's choral repertoire is intended for large performing forces and concert hall audiences. Berlioz' *Requiem* was first presented by nine hundred singers and instrumentalists. Many works, such as Beethoven's *Choral Symphony,* are primarily orchestral pieces requiring very large choruses for climactic impact.

But some Romanticists also wrote choral music of extraordinary beauty for more conservatively sized vocal groups. Many such works by Brahms are best performed by small chamber ensembles; motets by Bruckner fare better with somewhat larger forces. You should consider the expressive demands of these compositions on an individual basis when you are determining the appropriate number of singers.

2. *Stylistic requirements.*

- *Tonal color.* Expressive terms such as con fuoco (with fire) and mesto (sad) are indicative of the more emotional involvement required for the performance of Romantic period music. Singers need to produce a relatively more weighted and richer tonal quality. Beware, however, of oversinging, as evidenced by tense necks and, occasionally, red faces.

- *Phrasing.* Phrases are often irregular and frequently unpredictable. Concise phrases may be followed by others that are extended through the use of deceptive cadences or even absorbed into new material. Therefore, considerably more flexibility in breathing will be required. The director's prime responsibility in this regard is to show singers how individual phrases are to be interpreted.

- *Dynamics.* Changes in volume are sometimes abrupt and extreme. Dynamics may range from *pppp* to *ffff*, and a variety of levels are usually specified within a choral work. In these instances simply singing loud or soft will not satisfy requirements. For this reason, plan to spend time with your ensemble developing a full repertoire of individual dynamic levels. Changes in loudness also require subjective involvement by the singers for full impact. Pianissimos are best performed with hushed intensity; sudden fortissimos should be unleashed with emotional vigor.

- *Tempo.* Strictly regulated speed and moderate pace are not characteristic of the period. Terms such as presto and molto lento are common. Much of the choral repertoire requires a give-and-take in tempo. This is frequently requested by the composer in the form of accelerandos and ritardandos. In many other instances no markings are evident, yet some amount of phrasal freedom is obviously necessary to breathe life into melodic lines. Tempo rubato is an important interpretive refinement not to be overlooked when you are performing Romantic period music.

    3. *Interpretation.* Details in interpretive requirements differ among Romantic composers. For example, grace notes found in Schubert's vocal music are usually lengthened into eighth notes, whereas those encountered in Brahms' *Liebeslieder Waltzes* are performed more crisply so as not to interfere with the dance-like flow of the music. It is impossible to cover here the wide variety of interpretive nuances required for various composers' works. Score analysis will often reveal logical solutions. Critical listening of definitive performances will also lead to insights.

Impressionism

During the late nineteenth and early twentieth centuries, the French movement called "Impressionism" produced, among other things, several significant choral works. The chief composer of this late Romantic period trend was Claude Debussy. Choral directors should also note the works of Ravel and Delius, an Englishman who wrote in the same style.

In contrast to the predominantly assertive nature of most nineteenth century works, Impressionistic music hints rather than states, often becoming preoccupied with dreamlike evocation of moods. Melodic lines usually tend to avoid sharp contour or strong sense of direction. Pentatonic and whole-tone scales are extensively employed for flavor as well as to avoid the decisiveness of tonality. Harmony is often nonfunctional, relying for its effect on unresolved dissonances and parallel movement of "gliding chords." Even rhythm is generally subdued and stripped of any sense of momentum.

1. *Performers.* Some Impressionistic works, such as Delius' *Sea Drift,* require full orchestra and chorus. More intimate choral chansons by Ravel and Debussy are intended for a cappella performance by chamber-sized groups.

2. *Stylistic requirements.*

- *Tonal color.* Discipline and restraint are prerequisites for properly performing Impressionistic music. Controlled soft singing, requiring continual breath support, will aid in this regard if it is practiced and incorporated into the repertoire at hand. Even crescendos and dynamic climaxes should be conditioned by this regulated approach. Vibrato may be allowed to color vocal performance as with Romantic period repertoire.

- *Phrasing.* Impressionistic music is, for the most part, very flowing. Phrases are often irregular or fragmented to achieve this effect. Therefore, legato singing and unobtrusive breathing must permeate interpretive performance. Occasional deviations toward crisper articulation, as required in the music, should be conditioned by this basically smooth mode of presentation.

- *Dynamics.* Color, rather than stress and accent, has priority. For this reason, dynamics are more subdued and require appropriate restraint.

3. *Interpretation.* Impressionistic music is refined in construction and expressive detail. A considerable amount of polishing time will be needed for developing interpretive nuance. Singers need to

learn how to suggest rather than affirm in this style of musical expression.

TWENTIETH CENTURY MUSIC

Choral literature from the modern era presents an unprecedented challenge for today's ensemble director. Unlike music of earlier periods, many contemporary compositions require their own unique stylistic interpretation. This is especially true where composers have made significant changes in their compositional style. Keeping in mind that a twentieth century work must often be regarded as a law unto itself, you can still identify three general categories of choral repertoire requiring somewhat similar methods of interpretation.

Expressionism

Expressionistic music is, for the most part, atonal and usually implies the use of twelve-tone technique. Canonic devices, such as retrograde and inversion, are frequently used to present the original tone row in various forms. Representative choral composers are Schoenberg and Webern.

This type of music depends on distortion for its emotional impact. Excitement is created not only through pungent texts, but also by unusual musical surprises such as sporadic and unpredictable rhythms. Melodic lines often consist of jagged leaps distributed between vocalists and instrumentalists. Harmonic treatment is achieved primarily through the use of dissonant tone clusters.

1. *Performers.* Webern's cantatas are short, intensive works requiring chamber orchestra and small chorus for clarity. Stravinsky's *Threni,* on the other hand, is a more weighty composition, written for extensive performing forces. Expressionistic music is very demanding of singers. Technically it calls for extensive vocal range and unusual flexibility. Musically it requires excellent ears to locate and hold onto seemingly unrelated pitches. Performance of this music should only be attempted by advanced ensembles.

2. *Stylistic requirements.*

- *Pitch.* Unless the composer requests *Sprechstimme* (song speech), pitches must be performed exactly as written, or the music will lose its integrity and sense of character. Clarity of individual tones is essential, so vibrato must be kept to a minimum. Abundant time must be provided for note learning until singers gain confidence in locating and holding their pitches. Choristers should be encouraged to sing with relaxed jaws when they are negotiating wide intervallic leaps.

- *Phrasing.* Phrases are frequently constructed from strings of isolated notes and clusters distributed between various vocal parts and instruments in hocket style. Once the overall amount of give-and-take in rhythm and tempo has been determined for each phrase, performers must learn to come in at proper times so as not to destroy phrasal character.

- *Dynamics.* Sudden gushes of loudness followed by retreats into softness permeate the Expressionistic repertoire. Singers should be prepared to explode dynamic climaxes when necessary.

- *Tempo.* Speeds often fluctuate considerably over short spaces of time, a characteristic requiring flexibility on the part of the director and ready compliance by performers. In spite of highly angular vocal lines, rhythm must be scrupulously maintained, or the intensity in this type of music may be lost.

3. *Interpretation.* Expressionism often has a restless, even erotic quality which needs to be brought out in performance. Understanding and careful articulation of the text, with emotionalized emphasis of key words, will help in conveying appropriate mood.

Tonal-Oriented Music

A large proportion of twentieth century choral repertoire maintains some type of a relationship with tonality.

- Tonal-centered music creates a vague rather than definite sense of key.

- Polytonal music makes use of more than one key at the same time.

Common compositional devices encountered are primitive rhythms, chords built out of fourths, and jazz elements. Two compositional schools are represented within this category, each requiring somewhat different methods of interpretation.

NEOCLASSICISM

In an attempt to avoid both the unrestrained emotion of Romanticism and the exaggerated distortion of Expressionism some composers have combined contemporary technique with seventeenth and eighteenth century concepts and forms. Emphasis on craftsmanship and an objective style is usually the result. Contrapuntal composition, a prominent practice of this school, frequently employs harmonic dissonance through the use of highly independent lines. Rhythm plays an active, stylized role, as it did in the Classic period, but is often subjected to syncopation and metrical alteration. Leading composers of choral music in this style have included Stravinsky, Hindemith, Poulenc, and Britten.

1. *Performers*. Use of older genres such as the madrigal and cantata are indicative of the preference for smaller performing forces in Neoclassic music. Instruments are frequently placed in a chamber or solo role. Because of this increased responsibility, younger players may require additional guidance by the director.

2. *Stylistic requirements*. As with earlier period choral music, clarity of line is essential. Emotional expression should also be minimized in keeping with the more objective nature of this music.

3. *Interpretation*. Unlike Baroque and Classic period music, Neoclassic music provides little latitude for improvisation. Composers tend to specify their interpretive requirements with clarity and detail through the use of expressive terms and metronome markings.

NEO-ROMANTICISM

Twentieth century composers have also taken a different direction by incorporating their contemporary techniques within more sonorous forms characteristic of the Romantic period. Neo-Romantic choral works tend to emphasize textual content and subjective dramatic expression. A healthy proportion of this repertoire also contains elements of folk music, as exemplified by choral compositions of Kodály and Vaughan-Williams. Harmony is often of a less complex nature than harmony of late nineteenth century music. Yet it frequently produces rich colors with a sense of directness.

1. *Performers*. As in the Romantic period, choral works for large forces predominate. *Belshazzar's Feast* by William Walton,

scored for double chorus, orchestra, and two brass bands, is a prime example. However, excellent compositions for smaller groups also exist, including an abundance of selections for men's and women's ensembles.

2. *Stylistic requirements.* Neo-Romantic compositions require warmth and subjective expression, in keeping with nineteenth century interpretive practice. Many of these works, especially those written for small groups, depend heavily on mood for their success. The director should carefully choose tempos which best capture the work's expressive qualities.

Experimental Music

All twentieth century interpretive styles not previously discussed are included within this final category. Most experimental music offers increased interpretive responsibility for the performer. In some choral works this will mean that singers may choose their notes with certain latitude; in other instances individuals may perform their part with liberal freedom. Electronic music has also played an influential role in these types of choral compositions. Usually the choral group is backed in performance by electronic accompaniment played on a tape recorder.

1. *Performers.* Composers frequently leave ensemble size up to the director. This means that a particular work will take on different qualities depending on choice of performing forces. In these instances you should weigh the importance of clarity versus dynamic weight in determining the best solution for a particular work. Of course, other compositions may be more specific in their performance force requirements.

Composers also write for unusual combinations of voices and instruments. For example, *The Odes of Shang* by Seymour Shiffrin requires an extensive battery of percussive instruments including wind chimes and gongs.

2. *Stylistic requirements.* Tonal colors may vary from absolutely straight tones to dark, resonant speaking sounds. Dynamics often range in intensity from whispers to shouts. When they are performing microtones or even minor seconds, singers have a natural tendency to match notes with each other because they have been conditioned by tonal music. Time must be spent teaching them how to

select and maintain random pitches. A similar problem exists when they are attempting to perform irregular entries. Giving deliberately vague cues and showing individuals how to choose their own entries within time frames will help in this regard.

　　3. *Interpretation.* Because experimental music is so innovative, it is sometimes difficult to understand. Listeners must rely on effective performance if they are to gain an appreciation for this type of music. And successful presentations only result when singers are able to contribute with their understanding and commitment. Therefore, it is up to the director to provide his ensemble with a clear concept of an individual work's sense of purpose, mood, and format. Once this is established, performers must work with the director in experimenting with various types of articulation and timing until sounds, rhythmic patterns, and textures are found which best communicate the expressive content of a particular composition.

8

How to Prepare
the Conductor's Score

EXAMINING AND ANALYZING THE MUSICAL BLUEPRINT

What the Score Communicates

The musical score is a visual representation of the composer's creative ideas. In many ways, it is similar to an architect's blueprint.

- It conveys an overall design or form.
- It shows the materials chosen and offers a view of their relationships.
- It indicates directions for actual implementation.

By examining the score, the choral director can determine the music's overall logic. Such insight is a prerequisite both for planning effective rehearsals and for performing the work with clarity and meaning.

The *general* character of a musical composition is determined by three things:

- Function
- Form
- Sense of movement or direction

The work's *specific* character is influenced by the composer's choice of ingredients and a personalized treatment which makes the music truly unique. If the choral director is to gain a total understanding of these distinctive qualities, he must study the score in a process which moves from general familiarity to critical examination.

Becoming Acquainted with the Score

The familiarization phase begins even *before* the music is actually chosen for performance. Pre-selection factors such as repertoire need, available performers, and level of difficulty are considered. Reference copies are perused for textual content, individualistic features, and aesthetic impression. As a rule, the decision to perform any music should not be made until you have a clear picture of the work's actual suitability. This can be accomplished by studying the score silently, playing it on the keyboard, or listening to a recording.

After a choral composition has been chosen, the next step is to identify the following general features:

- Genre (madrigal, cantata, and so on)
- General style (Renaissance, Classical, and so on)
- Approximate performance time
- Meter
- Tempo

The third, and last, step in this initial familiarization phase is to determine the tonal structure of the work. Note that the word "key" is not used here, because much of the exciting choral music available for programming is written in "unconventional" sonoric idioms. Here is a list of tonal structures:

- Diatonic—major
- Diatonic—minor
- Modal
- Whole-tone
- Chromatic
- Atonal
- Polytonal (more than one key used *simultaneously*)
- Bifocal (*alternate* use of two keys)
- Tonal centered (creates only a *general* sense of key)
- Migrantly tonal (*alternate* use of tonality and atonality)
- Exotic

Examining the Score for Overall Form and General Content

In moving toward a more analytical phase, your next objective is to determine the work's basic construction. As in observing the layout of a building or the design of a product, this is achieved by locating sections and determining their relative proportions and substance. To assist in this process, a Form and Content Chart should be prepared. (See Figure 8-1.)

Lengthy choral works, such as oratorios, cantatas, and Masses, are usually composed in movements which should be compared for similarities and contrasts based on an analysis of each formal unit. Searching for sectional changes within these movements and in shorter works is best achieved by observing the following warning signs:

- Changes in key, meter, and tempo
- Completion of a textual idea or narrative episode
- Introduction of a new theme or contrasting melodic material
- Logical groupings of musical phrases and final cadences
- Contrasting uses of rhythm and harmony
- Changes in performing forces

When you are constructing the Form and Content Chart, be sure that these indicators are also noted. They will help provide clues to the next step, which is to evaluate the chart and determine the score's overall formal design. If you compare sections for similarities and contrasts, the music will most likely fall into one of the following categories:

- Strophic (a a a, etc.)
- Modified strophic (a a^1 a, etc.)
- Variation (a a^1 a^2, etc.)
- Stanza-refrain (a r b r, etc.)
- Binary ($|$: a :$|$: b :$|$)
- Ternary (a b a)
- Rounded binary ($|$: a :$|$: b a :$|$)
- Rondo (a b a c a, etc.)
- Imitative (fugue, canon)
- Through-composed (a b c d, etc.)
- Modified through-composed (a b c a, etc.)

FORM AND CONTENT CHART

Johannes Brahms. "Am Donaustrande," No. 9, from **Liebeslieder Walzer**, Op. 52

	5 10 15	20 25 30	35 40 45	50 55 60	65 70
MEASURES	1–18=18	19–34=16	: 35–47=13	48–62=15 :	63-64=2
METER	3/4 ───►				
TEMPO	"Ländler" ───►				
KEY	E Major ─────────────────►		B Major – g # minor	E Major ─────────►	
TEXT	Am Donaustrande .... Mädchen aus.	Das Mädchen ist .... Türe gelegt.	Zehn eiserne .... von Glas.	Am Donaustrande .... Mädchen aus.	
MELODIC LINE	2-phrased melody	Same, but with modified ending	New melodic material	Original melody	
VOCAL FORCES	A, T, B ───────────────────►		S, A, T, B	A, T, B	
ACCOMPANIMENT	Piano, for 4 hands Embellishing activity in upper part	Embellishing activity in lower part	Use of staccato in both parts	Embellishing activity shared between parts	──────────►
DYNAMICS	p ──────────────────────►		f	p	pp
SECTION DESIGNATOR	a	a'	: b	a :	piano ending

FORM: Rounded binary, commonly known as minuet form.

Figure 8-1

Interpreting the Text

The text usually provides a composer with the initial inspiration to create a new choral work. In this respect, the words are really the "backbone" of the composition. An understanding of key words and phrases as well as a grasp of the work's textual message will often provide insights to the music's phrase structure and expressive meaning. Furthermore, this knowledge, if it is conveyed to the singers, will make the difference between mere transmission of sounds and communication of feeling.

This discussion recalls an interesting personal experience. I once presented a choral work, based on a well-known storybook subject, to my choir for learning. After the initial run-through, some of the members complained about the sinister text, the clashing dissonances, and the general somberness of the music. The choir returned to the composition with a new-found enthusiasm after they were given pertinent insight. What was the music? It was Irving Fine's witty setting of the "Lullaby of the Duchess" from *Alice's Adventures in Wonderland*.

If you choose to perform foreign languages, do not rely exclusively on free translations to interpret the text. Word-for-word, verbatim translations usually provide insights that more poetical translations overlook. The intimate relationship between word and music in foreign music can often be appreciated only by digging into a translation dictionary for exact meaning.

MUSIC'S CHARACTER TRAITS

Clarifying Distinctive Qualities

Musical works can be compared to people's faces. Each is, somehow, different from the rest. Yet one is usually recognized from the other without conscious awareness of distinctive features. Choral directors, however, cannot accept such a passive role in their approach to interpreting a composition. The essence of a vivid performance lies in the ability of the conductor to clarify those distinctive qualities which give life to a musical work. Only in this sense do the director and his performers achieve the role of re-creators.

The unique character of a composition may be traced to a particular device or element. But often it is a combination of features which determines this individuality. Only by systematically looking at all aspects of the composer's work will these character traits become evident.

Introducing Character Analysis

Character Analysis is an organized method of examining all aspects of a musical work to determine its unique personality. Character analysis differs from theoretical analysis in that its goals are more performance oriented. If you follow its step-wise approach, a thorough understanding of the score is ensured.

To save time and minimize effort, the character analysis procedure is presented in worksheet form. Four of the fundamental elements of music—sound (also called timbre), melody, harmony, and rhythm—provide the basic avenues of concentration in this practical approach. Each is represented by a checklist. You should comb through the score for the information requested and make note of pertinent features. In some cases the characteristic searched for will not exist. It must be kept in mind, however, that the features which a work lacks as well as those it possesses are what give a composition its distinctive character.

THE CHARACTER ANALYSIS WORKSHEET

1. Analyze the overall sound.

    - Unusual individual or group performing forces
    - Unusual individual or group ranges or extremes
    - Frequency of timbral contrasts (shifts from high to low performing forces, changes between different sounding combinations, and so on)
    - Exploitation of singers or instruments for unusual effects
    - Types of articulation required (methods of attack, accentuation, and so on)
    - Types of dynamics indicated. Choose from the following:
        Terraced (abrupt)
        Tapered (gradual)
        Combination of the above
    - Frequency of implied dynamics resulting from addition or subtraction of performers or changes in range
    - Echo effects
    - Predominant dynamic level
    - Prevailing texture. Choose from the following:
        Homophony (chordal)
        True polyphony (contrapuntal)
        Harmonically-saturated polyphony
        Melody-bass polarity
        Melody and accompaniment

2. Analyze the melodic content.

    - Melodic design. Choose from the following:
        Motific (short, concise melodic figure)
        Thematic (subject of fugue or complete musical idea)
        Melodic (expanded linear material of three or more
            phrases)
        Combination of the above
    - Overall profile, or contour, of the melodic design.
      Evaluate for peaks and valleys.
    - Characteristic motion of the melodic design. Analyze for
      relative abruptness or gentleness in rise and fall.
    - Prevalence of steps, skips, or leaps
    - Use of question (antecedent) phrases and answer (conse-
      quent) phrases

3. Analyze the harmony.

    - General harmonic structure. Use the following procedure:
        a. Locate maximum harmonic tension and places
            of vertical complexity (active and dissonant
            chords, delayed resolutions, chord clusters, in-
            creased doubling, and so on).
        b. Locate areas of repose and vertical simplicity
            (final cadences, consonances, triads, minimal
            doubling, and so on).
    - Characteristic harmonic rhythm (general rate of harmonic
      change)
    - Use of compositional devices. Choose from the following:
        Circle of fifths
        Ostinato patterns
        Pedal point
        Arpeggio treatment
        Raised and lowered thirds
        Open (incomplete) chords
    - Unusual doublings, inversions, and progressions
    - Unusual implied harmonies

4.   Analyze the rhythm.

- Relationship of pulsation (underlying level of temporal activity) to meter
- Relationship between rhythm and meter. Choose from the following:
  Regular recurrence of rhythmic accent with metrical stress (isometrical rhythm)
  Independent rhythm with little or no dependence on metrical organization (multimetrical rhythm)
  Combination of the above
- Use of polyrhythm (*simultaneous* employment of two or more *independent* rhythmic patterns)
- Intensification and relaxation of rhythmic activity
- Use of compositional devices. Choose from the following:
  Augmentation
  Diminution
  Perpetual motion
  Rubato
  Hemiola
  Syncopation
- Relationship of rests to rhythmic structure
- Types of stress. Choose from the following:
  Natural (bar line)
  Dynamic induced (accent markings)
  Combination of the above
- Patterns of change in tempo and meter

TROUBLE-SHOOTING FOR POTENTIAL PROBLEMS

Foresight Saves Valuable Rehearsal Time

The effective choral director must anticipate potential problems encountered by singers learning and performing a musical work. He must either alleviate the obstacle completely or come up with a method of overcoming it with a minimum of rehearsal time and effort. Strictly vocal problems are discussed in the next chapter. Many problems, however, can be directly linked to the composition itself.

Choosing the proper remedy is as important to the trouble-shooting process as locating the problem. Sometimes good intentions in pinpointing potential pitfalls are defeated by ineffectual solutions. The ability to match obstacles with suitable antidotes is a hard-earned skill requiring common sense, imagination, experience, and sometimes trial-and-error testing. Here are a few general guidelines:

- Adopt a clinical approach by choosing a "tailor-made" prescription for each problem.
- Isolate the components in complex problems and tackle each aspect individually.
- Choose vocal demonstration whenever possible.
- Minimize theoretical discussions. The ear works better than the word.

Potential problems often become evident as the score is analyzed for its form, general content, and character traits. Others must be discovered through concentrated trouble-shooting. All tend to fall into three main categories:

- Reading problems
- Intonational problems
- Technical problems

Reading Problems

Many of the perplexities related to initial learning of the music can be traced to score reading. In searching for possible solutions, you should ask four basic questions of the score:

1. *Does the printed music hinder the performer?* Despite the authority of the printed note, mistakes *do* occur. Some publishers, unfortunately, have a reputation for allowing such blemishes to creep into their music. A typical example occurs when a chromatically altered note is not changed in all performance lines. Often this discrepancy occurs between the choral parts and the accompaniment.

Awkward page turns sometimes cause inconveniences at first. Cautioning singers to place a finger at that point for a fast turn will remedy the problem.

Occasionally, the notation or text is squeezed together to the point of creating a "sight reading traffic jam." The only solution is to slacken tempo until the performers become more familiar with the score.

2. *Does the score contain places where the singers may lose their musical frame of reference?* Much has been written about difficulties in sight reading. Most occur simply because the singer does not sense the relationship of his part to the total ensemble. Finding initial pitches, modulating to new keys, and confidently progressing through dissonances can only be achieved when the performer hears his part contextually.

The role of the choral director in providing musical reference points cannot be overstressed. Sometimes this may mean locating common tones between two parts; in other instances, clarifying harmonic progressions will help. Often these reference points can only be discovered by patiently studying the score.

3. *Is the music unpredictable?* Altered sequences, sudden contrasts in harmonic treatment, and abrupt dynamics are examples of favorite compositional surprises. Singers will sometimes fall into these musical pitfalls unless they are forewarned.

4. *Are there speed traps?* Highly energized rhythmic passages such as those typically found in Baroque contrapuntal music pose sight-reading obstacles to the average singer. Chordal music marked by unrestful skips and leaps within vocal lines poses similar problems. Generally speaking, clusters of short-durational notes, busy chromatic activity, and intensified vertical movement indicate speed traps. The solution? Treat the tempo conservatively at first.

Intonational Problems

Pitch problems caused by faulty vocal technique and hearing are discussed in the next two chapters. Intonation is also affected by acoustical conditions created by the musical composition.

1. *Look for individual notes which control tonal structure.* Leading tones, especially when they are employed for modulation to a new key, cannot be allowed to sag. The third of a chord must be sung with precision because it determines the mode of the chord. Notes which change the character of a sequence are also important. If not performed properly, sequential passages will sound muddy and ambiguous.

2. *Treat unison passages with caution.* From the standpoint of

pitch, a choral ensemble is *naked* whenever it performs music in unison or at the octave. Watch for cadences ending with such treatment.

Technical Problems

These obstacles range from simple clarification of musical terminology to matters of syncronization. Technical problems tend to fall into the following three categories:

1. *Problems in clarification.* What does "Bocca chiusa" mean? How does one perform a Baroque trill? Scores are often filled with symbols and directions unfamiliar to the choral member. Based on a knowledge of your group, you must be prepared to provide information and insights to the extent that *all* musical data contained in the composition can be translated into accurate performance.

2. *Breathing problems.* Every score requires a "plan of attack" for breathing. Nothing destroys the momentum or mood of a work more than obtrusive sounds of rushing air in the wrong places. A lengthy musical arc may demand staggered breathing. Conversely, the repetition of a textual statement or individual word may require interjection of breaths or pauses. The conscientious director will test his breathing plan by singing through the score *before* presenting it to the ensemble.

3. *Coordination problems.* All music contains primary and subsidiary activity. For example, the subject of a fugue is passed about while other voices provide the countersubject or free material. The discerning director must plan to control performance balances based on an analysis of this musical activity. Duplicate responses require equal balance. Yet, if the chorus is hampered by unequal vocal strength between sections of the ensemble, modification of dynamics or substitution of voices may be necessary.

Trouble-shooting may also reveal relatively independent movement between vocal lines. Renaissance madrigals characteristically employ this treatment. Be sure that this type of music does not "loosen at the seams" by carefully regulating the tempo.

MARKING THE SCORE

This last step in score preparation is absolutely essential, for it allows you to clearly observe and communicate important information found on the printed page of music. Many directors, however, limit themselves by using one color. When you employ various colors, you will be able to glance at your score and immediately see critical markings, points of information, and so on.

Several color codes are possible. Once you have chosen a system, stay with it in all score marking and you will begin to react automatically to the various colors as they are approached in rehearsing or performing. I prefer the following color code:

1. *Yellow* is ideal for highlighting all tempo, metric, and key markings. It is also good for bringing out interpretation and articulation terms and markings.

2. *Blue* works well for various piano dynamic markings and decrescendos. I differentiate between levels of softness by varying the shape of my markings.

   - $\widehat{pp}$
   - $\widehat{p}$
   - $\boxed{mp}$

3. *Red* is a logical choice for all forte markings and crescendos. The various levels of loudness can also be set off by varying the shape of your colored markings.

   - $\boxed{mf}$
   - $\widehat{f}$
   - $\widehat{ff}$

4. *Black* is good for writing in additional information such as places for breathing or new markings. Word and note changes as well as phonetic markings should also be written in black. Any of these additions could, in turn, be highlighted in yellow for further clarity.

5. *Green* is especially useful for writing in performer cues. Reminders for changing lighting, seating singers, and so on can also be included.

9

Working with the Human Voice

Successful choral directors have a "feel" for working with singers. There are, of course, instances where conductors unfamiliar with vocal techniques have managed to pull off polished performances. Usually, however, these successes result because of trained or enthusiastic singers and in spite of their leader's limitations.

Therefore, as a choral director you need to become intimately acquainted with the mechanics of singing. There are five specific reasons for this.

- So that you may obtain a wider repertoire of vocal expression from your singers
- So that these responses will be achieved with a minimum of vocal strain
- So that you will use vocal techniques which are compatible with standards of proper singing
- So that you will be aware of individual and ensemble vocal problems
- So that you may communicate better with your singers

CONTROL OF THE SINGING PROCESS

Singing Is a Cyclic Process

The act of singing requires continual adjustment by the singer. For each and every note attempted, the individual strives to accommodate vowel, pitch, and intensity in such a way as to produce his best tone quality. Sometimes this effort is unconscious, but it always occurs. The brain obviously must play a major role in this dynamic process by monitoring each sound and sensation and then by providing new signals for each ensuing tone. Singing is, therefore, a cyclic process comprised of mental and neurophysical activity. (See Figure 9-1.)

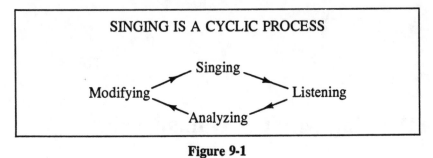

Figure 9-1

Looking at the above diagram, you can see how "all stages must be go" in order for proper singing to occur. As a matter of fact, the best voice teachers facilitate vocal development by providing helpful guidance and information at *each* stage of the cyclic process. You can also achieve superior ensemble results by placing yourself in a similar tactical position, providing helpful information for each of these stages. Here is how it works.

1. *The singing stage.* Any information provided by the choral director will become integrated into the entire cyclic process. On the other hand, highly specific technical instructions can result in direct vocal improvement without overloading the mental compo ents of the cycle. For example,

- If ensemble tone is faulty, diagnose the problem nd provide simple remedies ("Your high notes sound pinche ; sing them again as though you are yawning").

- Whenever enunciation needs improving, correct t with concise directions ("Round the 'oh' vowels more").

2. *The listening stage.* In some ways, this will b your most challenging area of vocal work. All musicians continually need to improve their listening perception. Singers have the double burden of locating exact pitch along a sliding scale and coming up with appro-

priate tone quality on an instrument with vast sonoric latitude. You can help your singers by taking two distinct approaches.

- By showing them *what* to listen for. Some examples would be clarity of tone, balance between sections, and proper intonation.
- By challenging them to listen more perceptively ("Basses, sing your part one step higher against the other voice parts!").

3. *The analytic stage.* In order for a singer to analyze his vocal contributions, he must have something to compare his efforts with. Such perspective usually comes from one's own previous singing experiences. Just as important, however, are those comparisons made with *outside* sources. You can perform an invaluable service by providing vocal models for your singers to match or emulate. When you demonstrate proper vocal production or praise instances of good ensemble singing, your choir members will begin to develop that perspective so necessary for musical growth. Here are some specific suggestions.

- Play recordings of superior and inferior performances and explain why they are so rated.
- Use individuals within the ensemble to demonstrate particular qualities you are trying to achieve.

4. *The modification stage.* Tied in closely with the actual act of singing, this component of the cyclic process depends on timely and accurate adjustments by the singer for success. Those "specific technical instructions" mentioned under "The singing stage" could just as well have been listed here. Of equal importance at this point is your control over the quantity of change made by the singers. You must act as a monitor by reacting to changes made by the ensemble.

- "When singing that pianissimo, you lost intensity as well as volume. Please maintain a supported tone even though you are singing softly."
- "There is not enough contrast between your legato and staccato singing. Try to exaggerate these differences."

I know that there are directors who tend to concentrate on one or two stages of the singing cycle and fail to consider the rest. Usually, this results in partial success. One such individual was masterful in improving tone quality through technical adjustment but rarely worked on listening perception. Consequently, his choral ensembles had a reputation for singing with a hearty, robust sound slightly out of tune!

Ensemble Performance Requires Teamwork

All choirs have their share of vocal leaders and followers. This is a natural and desirable thing as long as all work toward a well-balanced, cohesive product. The choral director's role in this regard is that of a catalyst, channeling individual efforts in the group's general direction.

This brings us to a discussion of soloists. In most instances, these individuals are able to make significant contributions without destroying the balance or blend of an ensemble. Occasionally, I have found it necessary to ask those with a healthy vibrato or projection to control their contributions. I also believe that there are instances in which a soloist should not be asked to join a choral organization. An exceptionally powerful and penetrating voice should not be expected to operate at half-speed. This is especially true for smaller chamber ensembles which, ironically, seem to draw the attention of soloists the most.

Sometimes a young singer has vocal problems which dictate special consideration. Just recently I restricted one of my altos to light singing in choir rehearsals because she was having range coordination problems in her voice lessons. After two weeks she regained her vocal balance and was permitted to resume normal singing.

Aside from such individual matters, keep in mind that your primary duty is to stress vocal teamwork. This means that all exercises and directions will be conditioned by consideration for group improvement. In fact, it is my belief that all successful choral directors secretly share the following motto:

Insistence on group vocal teamwork is the key to ensemble success.

How to Develop Expressive Freedom

Because singing is a highly personal art, individuals are usually reluctant to take chances vocally. This is especially true of beginners and shy singers. Yet, it is axiomatic that as people gain confidence, they begin to "stick their necks out." This means that you must find ways to instill this confidence by urging singers to make the gamble. Here are several tried-and-tested ways to develop expressive freedom.

- Choose vocal exercises which demand a variety of expressive moods.
- Use body movement exercises to promote a sense of physical freedom and well-being.
- Encourage musical response through enthusiastic, positive requests.
- Stress cooperative spirit.

DEALING WITH INDIVIDUAL VOICES AND THEIR CHARACTERISTICS

For the most part, it is possible to deal collectively with all singers in an ensemble and get good vocal results by using generalized techniques. For example, all choir members will benefit equally from breathing exercises, regardless of voice type. Sooner or later, however, you will be required to solve a problem for an individual section of voices.

This is especially true for conductors who direct contrasting groups such as a men's glee club or a women's ensemble. Not long ago, I had an interesting conversation with another choral director whose school had recently become coeducational. He said that he felt comfortable working with boys' voices but didn't know how to get a good sound from his recently formed girls' ensemble. Experience is, of course, a crucial factor, but a knowledge of voice types and their characteristics is also invaluable.

The Soprano Voice

1. *Range* (optimum range for more mature voices given in brackets)

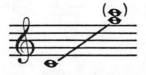

First Soprano

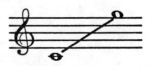

Second Soprano

2. *Tessitura*

First Soprano   Second Soprano

3. *Ideal qualities:* Flutelike sound; buoyancy and agility
4. *Undesirable tendencies:* Shrillness; thinness of tone; breathiness

The Alto Voice

1. *Range*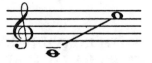

First Alto   Second Alto

2. *Tessitura*

First Alto   Second Alto

3. *Ideal qualities:* Round, full-bodied sound; mellowness
4. *Undesirable tendencies:* Hootiness; wobble

The Tenor Voice

1. *Range*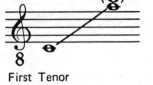

First Tenor   Second Tenor

2. *Tessitura*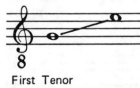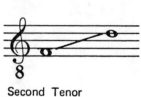

First Tenor   Second Tenor

3. *Ideal qualities:* Lyricism; head voice

4. *Undesirable tendencies:* Blatant, pushed-up high notes; pinched sound

The Bass Voice

1. *Range*

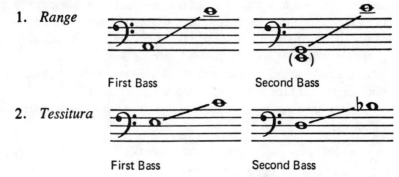

First Bass   Second Bass

2. *Tessitura*

First Bass   Second Bass

3. *Ideal qualities:* Resonant supporting tones; exactness of pitch

4. *Undesirable tendencies:* Boominess; unwieldy sounds

The "In-Between Voice": How to Make the Best of It

Occasionally you will find singers whose compass of singable notes falls smack in between two choral parts. This situation usually occurs with mezzo-sopranos and baritones of limited range. These individuals should not be avoided because they cannot be pigeonholed into a preconceived vocal category. Quite often, they may be utilized effectively as what I call "swivel chairs." For example, a young baritone who cannot reach lower notes may be assigned to the bass section with the following instructions:

- Sing low notes beyond your reach up an octave.
- Sing the tenor part in places where additional support is needed.
- Always sing the upper line in divisi bass scoring.

Sometimes one comes across fortunate vocalists who can reach all of the notes in two or more vocal parts. Where should they be placed? The answer is simple: where they will be most comfortable. During the initial audition, time should be spent with these singers to determine exactly where their tessitura lies. This will be the deciding factor.

WHAT TO DO ABOUT VOCAL HYGIENE

Some choral directors take what I call a "passive attitude" toward their singers' vocal health. That is, they provide no guidance or precautions regarding vocal hygiene. Then, when their performers become ill or vocally indisposed, they blame these circumstances on bad luck. It is certainly true, of course, that little can be done when a flu epidemic hits an entire school. Nevertheless, there are specific steps a choral director should take to minimize vocal casualties.

Here are three approaches which I have found to be particularly effective.

- Provide singers with a health checklist.
- Watch for faulty singing.
- Work around vocal ailments.

Provide Singers with a Health Checklist

The best way to avoid poor health or ailments is by establishing a preventative maintenance program. Younger singers are sometimes willing to take chances by running around in cold weather without a coat, shouting at December football games, and so on. If you can get the point across that healthy singers are essential to a good choral ensemble, then you might be able to establish a foothold in preventing unnecessary vocal and health disorders. One effective way to accomplish this is by providing each vocalist with a Health Checklist. This short list of items can be taped into choir folders and will serve as a constant reminder to keep fit. (See Figure 9-2.)

Watch for Faulty Singing

Some of my fondest memories go back to my early days as a member of a college fraternity. Inevitably, there was the late Saturday night songfest. I will never forget those red faces—and the Sunday morning sore throats which everyone seemed to complain about. Those carefree days at least taught me a lesson about singing, and I try to make sure that my singers do not fall into the same trap. Here are some warning signs of improper vocal production.

- Poor posture, especially a sagging chest
- Tight jaw
- Closed throat
- Tense tongue

The astute choral director will "nip the problem in the bud" through effective remedies. To improve sitting posture, ask your singers to stand and then sit on the edge of their seats without changing the erectness of their upper torsos. Tenseness and tightness can be eliminated by introducing loosening-up exercises. Sometimes singers tend to pinch their vowels in a particular musical work. In this case, continual encouragement to keep the vowels open will help to offset improper singing.

HEALTH CHECKLIST

- Get enough sleep
- Eat properly
- Dress adequately
- Avoid shouting
- Keep neck covered in cold weather
- Avoid cold liquids before and during singing
- Stay dry in wet weather
- Do not sing with sore throat

Figure 9-2

Work Around Vocal Ailments

Many a singer has lost an inordinate amount of rehearsal and performance time because one of the following situations occurred:

- The singer was overenthusiastic and tried to sing in spite of a severe vocal disorder.
- The conductor was oblivious to the singer's problem or failed to insist on sufficient recuperation time.

Choral directors are not doctors, but there are steps we should take whenever a "battlefield casualty" occurs.

- Recognize the symptoms and nature of the ailment.
- Be prepared to make an objective decision regarding the indisposed singer's immediate relationship with the ensemble.

For minor vocal inconveniences this may mean asking the member to sing lightly. Those hampered by more severe disorders might attend rehearsals to learn their music but refrain from singing. Severe cases obviously would require complete absence from rehearsals. The common vocal ailments are listed below in order of their severity.

1. *Hoarseness.* Partial loss of the voice accompanied by irritation. Usually the full voice returns again by the next day. Hoarseness occurs most frequently at the beginning of the singing year. First signs are wheezing cough and weeping eyes. At the outset, the singers should take a break and then sing softly upon return. If hoarseness persists, the individual should be given the entire rehearsal off.

2. *Common cold.* Viral attack on the respiratory system, resulting in runny nose and sneezing. Statistics show that as many as 90 percent of your singers will catch a cold during the year, and over half of them will probably have several colds. "Three days coming, three days with you, and three days going" is an old but fairly accurate description of a typical cold cycle.

Unfortunately, the cold virus is highly communicable, and a hyperactive sneezer can contaminate an entire vocal section. As a general rule, try to give the more "advanced" cases time off, especially when concerts are not impending.

Vocalists with a cold can usually perform if they have to by "singing over" their imposition. This is achieved as follows:

- By relying on proper vocal coordination and not pushing their voices
- By experimenting with vocal sounds until they obtain maximum clarity for their condition. A relaxed open throat will help in this regard.

3. *Common sore throat.* Inflammation of the pharynx. Often these are mild, transient irritations occurring in conjunction with a cold

or as a result of catching a draft. Sore throats also serve as warnings for more serious ailments, particularly strep throat. Singers who complain should be closely watched and, preferably, should not sing. In some instances, this precaution will save them from from coming down with one of the next two incapacitating ailments.

4. *Pharyngitis*. Severe inflammation of the pharynx. Symptoms are significant pain in the throat causing difficulty in swallowing. Phlegm is often present. Under no circumstances should a singer perform with these symptoms. Pharyngitis usually lasts up to seven days.

5. *Laryngitis*. Inflammation of the larynx. This is the most severe of all vocal disorders. Complete loss of the voice for several days is common, but be prepared to lose your ensemble member for as long as two weeks. Progress in regaining the singing voice is slow. If speaking and singing are not approached gradually, a relapse may occur.

In addition to the vocal ailments described, singers suffer from other indispositions which limit their performing ability. Be especially on the lookout for the following problems:

- Respiratory allergies
- Swollen glands
- Toothaches
- Tonsillitis

Whenever any of your choral members run into vocal ailments, it is always a good idea to "touch base" with their voice teachers if they study privately. Individuals with severe problems will benefit by your persuasion to see an ear, nose, and throat specialist.

EXERCISING THE ENSEMBLE

It is my personal conviction that exercises can make or break an ensemble. Simply put, unless your singers are willing to apply themselves to *productive* vocal exercising, you will probably never reach group potential.

But, let's face it, for many directors warming up the choir seems to be a necessary evil. I must admit, I used to find the routine of "mulling through" several drills a boring experience. The singers were inevitably restless, and little seemed to be accomplished other than clearing vocal cobwebs. Then, I began to experiment and discovered some important facts.

- A planned variety of exercises made activities more interesting, and vocalists became better motivated.
- When the purpose of a new exercise was briefly explained, singers approached the task as a challenging game.
- The ensemble was just as easily warmed up through exercises which also dealt with specific group vocal problems.

Obviously, these changes have required me to expand my repertoire of exercises continually, often by creating new ones. The results, however, have more than justified my efforts.

Some Facts about Exercises

How do you know if an exercise is a good one? Here are several factors to consider when you are choosing or devising exercises.

1. *Exercises must adhere to fundamentals of proper singing.* Do not expect your tenors to hum pianissimo above a high G. Over a period of time the results would be disastrous. Similarly, one would not choose forte exercises which demand deep chest tones from your alto section. Good exercises allow the voice to blossom; bad exercises place undue stress on singing technique.

2. *Exercises must be applied clinically.* No one exercise will guarantee results just because it has proven to be successful for others. An exercise is like a prescription—it must be chosen as a remedy for an individual group at a particular time. Ensemble attitude, level of musical development, and vocal growth are some of the factors to be considered. Quite often a new vocal problem replaces an old one. To avoid or ignore these changes by continuing exercises which have lost their effectiveness or usefulness is to run the risk of stagnating your choral program.

3. *Whenever possible, exercises should be taken from actual music.* The primary reason for exercising is to prepare the vocal group for performance. This means that those exercises which come closest to helping singers perform their music better will have the most relevance. Figure 9-3 contains an exercise designed to improve vocal agility. It was derived from those demanding runs found in the *Messiah* chorus, "For unto Us a Child Is Born." By modulating the drill and

stressing proper articulation of each note, the ensemble will have less difficulty when it comes to actually performing Handel's work.

4. *Good exercises accomplish more than one objective.* The exercise period cannot take up an inordinate amount of rehearsal time, and good exercises save time by meeting primary and secondary vocal needs. For example, the exercise in Figure 9-4 is primarily designed to promote resonant sonority, yet it also gives singers the experience of singing whole tones with proper chordal intonation.

Planning Daily Exercises

As a general rule, exercise activities should be considered on a daily basis along with repertoire planning. This does not necessarily mean that new exercises will be chosen every day. Some are designed for long-range improvement, and to eliminate them suddenly might defeat their purpose. On the other hand, exercises which have grown stale or lost their effectiveness need replacing. When you are evaluating each day's activities, ask yourself the following questions:

- What vocal problems need to be corrected?
- What aspects of ensemble singing need improving?
- What performance problems exist within current and upcoming repertoire?
- What areas of general musicianship or mental alertness need attention?
- What steps should be taken, based on answers to the above questions, to change, add, or modify exercises for the next rehearsal?

The next step is to consider which types of exercises are needed to accomplish your objectives. All tend to fall into one of the following categories:

1. *Warm-up exercises.* These are designed to "wake-up" the singer and his voice so that repertoire demands will not be initially overtaxing. Note that physical activity may be included.

2. *Corrective exercises.* These remedial activities are intended to eliminate basic vocal problems shared by members of the ensemble. For example, faulty intonation would be improved through corrective exercises.

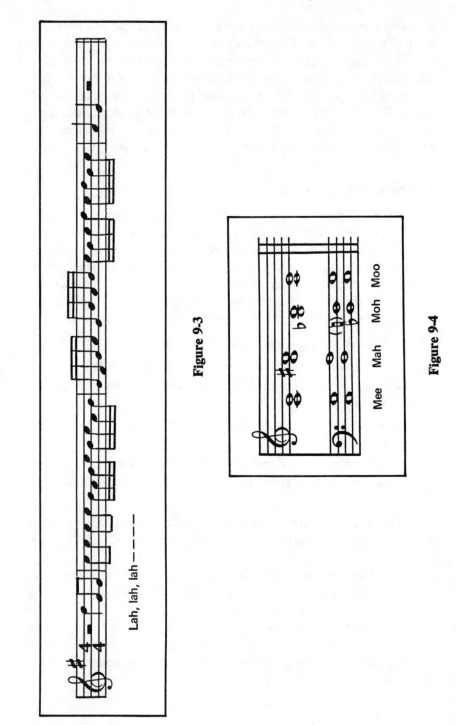

Figure 9-3

Lah, lah, lah -----

Mee   Mah   Moh   Moo

Figure 9-4

3. *Developmental exercises.* These serve as avenues for group improvement. They differ from corrective exercises in that they transform basically correct performance into superior response. Learning to sing with presence would be a developmental activity.

Some exercises which I have found to work particularly well are presented in the remainder of this chapter.

Warm-Up Exercises: An Ideal Procedure

Singing requires a high energy level both physically and mentally. For this reason an ideal warm-up procedure should incorporate physical and mental activities along with vocal exercises.

1. *Physical movement.* Before the voice itself can be "awakened," the body should be readied for action.

a. *Common problems.* Singers are often sleepy when they arrive for morning rehearsals, lethargic after lunchtime meals, and simply tired later in the day. In short, their energy level is usually inadequate. Posture also tends to deteriorate as the day progresses.

b. *Procedures.* Physical exercises should be designed to prepare singers for active participation. A feeling of physical looseness and ready coordination is promoted. Proper posture is achieved by alignment activities.

c. *Suggested exercises*

Objective No. 1: Proper posture. Singers stand tall and raise hands high over their heads. Arms are very slowly lowered while chest is kept in comfortably high position.

Objective No. 2: Invigoration. Singers turn to the right and rub each others' shoulders. They then turn to the left and repeat the procedure.

Objective No. 3: Body freedom. Singers spread out, place hands on hips, and take moderately wide stance. They then stretch at the waist by alternately bobbing upper torso to the left and to the right three times.

Objective No. 4: Activated breathing. Singers pronounce unvoiced consonants "f," then "s," and then "sh" in unison. Each consonant is aspirated sharply so that the diaphragm "kicks" for each sound. The exercise begins slowly at first, with no intervening pause between each "f-s-sh" sequence. The goal is to speed up the pace steadily without losing diaphragm support of each individual sound.

  2. *Mental activities*. Proper singing depends on getting clear signals from the brain. This, in turn, requires alertness and concentration.

   a. *Common problems*. Singers are not always in "the mental swing of things." Their aural perception may be sluggish. Often, initial vocal production is muddled by unclear thought patterns.

   b. *Procedures*. Singers must become immediately preoccupied with musical thinking and reacting. Concentration, critical listening, and flexibility are promoted through exercise "surprises."

   c. *Suggested exercises*

   Objective No. 1: Rhythmic perception. Director claps one measure of rhythm and then continues with new rhythms as ensemble imitates at one measure delay.

   Objective No. 2: Melodic perception. Director sings or plays on the keyboard one measure of melody and then continues with new melodic material as ensemble imitates at one measure delay.

   Objective No. 3: Musical memorization. Director places short melody on chalkboard. Singers perform and then study the music. Melody is erased, and singers perform from memory.

  3. *Vocalizing*. These exercises allow singers to ease into singing before tackling repertoire.

   a. *Common problems*. When not warmed up, singers tend to overexert their voices, sing with improper support, and perform with tenseness. Probably the most common problem is a tendency to sing with too much chest voice.

   b. *Procedures*. Exercises should begin at or near the pitch level of the speaking voice and then gradually extend outward toward more extreme ranges. A key factor is the initial emphasis on lyrical singing and a *gentle* settling into chest voice through downward vocalization.

c. *Suggested exercises* (in order of logical sequence)

Objective No. 1: Initial phonation. Singers perform five-note descending scale. (See Figure 9-5.) A relaxed, open throat is

Oh   woh woh woh woh

Figure 9-5

stressed. Begin the exercise in the middle range and move each sequence up by half steps until the beginning note is comfortably high. At this point, reverse the process by moving the sequence downward until the final note is comfortably low.

Objective No. 2: Controlled range extension. Singers perform arpeggiated-scalar exercise. (See Figure 9-6.) Dynamics and articulation require singers to use careful support and placement when they are ascending. Begin exercise in moderately low key and then move upward.

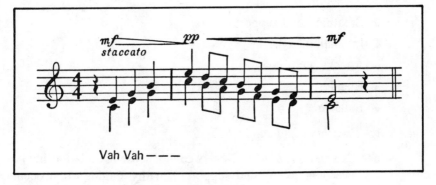

Vah Vah — — —

Figure 9-6

Use various vowels

Figure 9-7

Objective No. 3: Sustained tone singing. Singers perform chorale-type exercises such as Figure 9-7. Director emphasizes supported legato singing at various tempos and dynamic levels.

Corrective Exercises for Five Key Problem Areas

As was previously pointed out, exercises are extremely important for choral group success. And without a doubt their greatest value lies in remedying ensemble faults and weaknesses. The director's role in this regard cannot be overstressed. By trouble-shooting for inadequacies and providing corrective exercises, you can turn a problem-ridden choir into a smooth-running organization. This, of course, requires proper diagnosis. When listening carefully to the ensemble, you will find that the problems encountered fall under one of the following areas of concern:

- Breathing and support
- Intonation
- Attacks and releases
- Blend
- Balance

1. *Breathing and support*

a. *Common problems.* Singers cannot sense the relationship between breathing and support. Breathy singing often occurs because of an improperly regulated supply of air.

b. *Procedures.* Exercises which isolate the breathing and support mechanism are provided so that the individual may learn for himself how to control this aspect of singing.

c. *Suggested exercises*

Objective No. 1: Economy of air supply. Singers are instructed to take a deep breath by breathing "down and out." They then emit a long "pinpoint" hiss. Emphasize the need for a steady emission without surges in air intensity.

Objective No. 2: Energized support. Singers perform repetitions of chord (see Figure 9-8), releasing each note with a sharp grunt. This produces very active movement of the diaphragm. The exercise repeats the chord four times and then moves immediately up by half step without interruption.

Figure 9-8

2. *Intonation*

a. *Common problems.* Faulty pitch is usually caused by singers who either do not hear their part contextually or who have a vocal production problem inhibiting them from singing in tune.

b. *Procedures.* A cappella exercises which require singers to think with their inner ear work best. The director must insist on proper vowel formation and adequate support since these two factors are instrumental in maintaining proper intonation.

c. *Suggested exercises*

Objective No. 1: Inner ear development. Singers perform choral work until signalled to cease. They continue to read music silently until signalled to come in again. Repertoire will vary from simple unison melodies to difficult four-part works, depending on the group's level of development.

Objective No. 2: Chordal tuning. Singers begin chord. (See Figure 9-9.) Each section moves up by half step until entire chord has been modulated upward. Flow of continued sound is maintained by using staggered breathing.

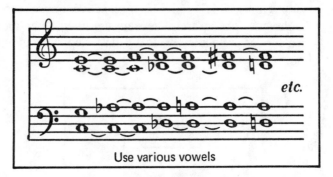

Figure 9-9

Objective No. 3: Interval recognition. Singers perform intervals in unison, as requested by the director. More advanced ensembles begin on a unison note; however, individual sections move to intervals when requested. These intervals may be prearranged by the director so as to maintain tonality. The use of seconds, tritones, and so on produce an atonal result.

3. *Attacks and releases*

a. *Common problems.* Ensemble does not sense point at which it should come in or cut off. Sometimes singers are partially impeded from coordinated attacks and releases by consonants, range, and dynamic levels.

b. *Procedures.* Simple chordal exercises allow singers to concentrate on attacks and releases while the director varies musical conditions.

c. *Suggested exercises*

Objective No. 1: Pinpoint entries and releases. Singers perform the word "toot" on single chord. Director varies tempo and dynamic levels. Emphasis on precise initial and final "t" is stressed.

Objective No. 2: Proper treatment of consonants. Singers perform various consonants and vowels on single chord. Director emphasizes rule of thumb that initial consonants *precede* point of entry cued by the conductor and final consonants are effected at point of release. Tempo, range, and dynamics are varied by the director.

Objective No. 3: Timely entries after rests. Singers perform repertoire containing lengthy rests for each choral part. The director does not cue entries but insists on accurate attacks by clapping the meter.

4. *Blend*

a. *Common problems.* Poor blend is sometimes caused by singers with excessive vibrato or shrillness of tone. Most instances, however, result simply because individuals lack ensemble awareness.

b. *Procedures.* Exercises which help to equalize voices by providing a common denominator work best. For example, concentrating on a single vowel and stressing uniformity of sound will allow individuals to become more sensitized in their ensemble relationship.

c. *Suggested exercises*

Objective No. 1: Uniform volume. Simple, four-part exercises are performed on single vowels molto legato. Controlled pianissimo singing is stressed at first. Singers are continually reminded that they must be able to hear their neighbors or they are singing too loud. Eventually, higher dynamic levels are introduced, but with emphasis on control.

Objective No. 2: Covered vowels. Simple chorales are used. Begin with humming and then ask singers to *gradually* move into a specific vowel without changing the quality of the tone. At first, use "back" vowels (oh, oo); later, allow singers to move into "forward" vowels (ah, eh, ee). To ensure continuity between the hum and vowels, have singers change back and forth within the chorale.

5. *Balance*

a. *Common problems*. Ensemble sections are often unequal in terms of dynamic weight. This lack of balance tends to be most noticeable at climactic passages.

b. *Procedures*. Balance problems are best eliminated by seating singers in quartets or repositioning sections so that individuals will begin to sense the relationship of their parts to others. Contrapuntal exercises are good for emphasizing equal loudness between sections when they are stating the subject and lesser volume when they are performing subordinate material.

c. *Suggested exercises*

Objective No. 1: Sectional awareness. While singers perform a chorale, the director continually experiments with balances by requesting one section to increase volume, another section to decrease volume, and so on.

Objective No. 2: Dynamic equality. Individual sections perform isolated notes at specific dynamic levels back and forth to each other. The singers note their "differences of opinion" and then, guided by the director, learn to match volume at each dynamic level.

Developmental Exercises

As was pointed out in Chapter 6, your choral ensemble's level of ability must be considered when you are choosing repertoire. Unfortunately, directors sometimes fall into one of two traps in this regard.

- They play it safe by always performing music well within the grasp of their ensemble. This approach stunts musical growth.
- They choose challenging repertoire but take a passive attitude toward this growth process, hoping that somehow the vocal group will meet the challenge.

The answer, of course, lies in choosing developmental exercises, either in conjunction with or in anticipation of more demanding repertoire, so that the choir may move forward with confidence and technical facility. These exercises tend to fall into one of the following categories:

- Range
- Agility
- Intensity
- Expression

1. *Range*

a. *Desirable goals.* Singers should be able to perform all notes encountered in their repertoire without jeopardizing ensemble blend and, more importantly, without incurring tenseness.

b. *Procedures.* Vocal ranges must be stretched without forcing by emphasizing coordination and placement rather than manipulation.

c. *Suggested exercises*

Objective No. 1: Cultivation of head voice. Singers perform descending octave scales glissando on "huh." (See Figure 9-10.) Initial high note is to be approached as a pinpoint entry. This is achieved by stressing high placement and support. Singers are cautioned not to sing heavier as they descend the scale. Move the exercise up by half steps.

Objective No. 2: Range extension. Singers perform "add-on exercise" by moving from one to two to three notes, and so on, always returning to "do," until a five-note scale is reached. (See Figure 9-11.) These scales ascend and are modulated upward for the development of high notes; then they descend and are modulated downward for the development of low notes.

2. *Agility*

a. *Desirable goals.* Singers need to develop sufficient vocal flexibility to perform fast-moving runs and wide intervals with accuracy.

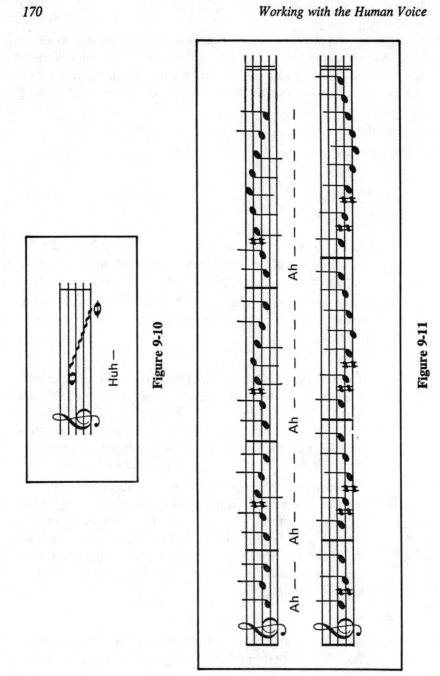

Figure 9-10

Figure 9-11

b. *Procedures.* Exercises used should allow singers to gradually increase tempo without sacrificing precise intonation. A variety of consonants will help in the articulation of individual notes.

c. *Suggested exercises*

Objective No. 1: Equal treatment of fast-moving runs. Singers perform staccato at moderate speed. (See Figure 9-12.) When the ensemble can perform the run with proper intonation and steady rhythm, the exercise is repeated at a faster pace.

Objective No. 2: Rapid adjustment to wide intervals. Singers perform arpeggio exercises such as the one suggested in Figure 9-13. Tempo is increased as the ensemble becomes more proficient in making accurate adjustments.

3. *Intensity*

a. *Desirable goals.* Singers should be able to produce and maintain an even sonority and richness of tone, especially when they are performing soft or low notes.

b. *Procedures.* Initial exercising should facilitate the development of intensity as a norm of singing. Later exercises should require singers to maintain this quality of singing under more demanding musical conditions.

c. *Suggested exercises*

Objective No. 1: Resonant sonority. Singers emphasize consonant "m" in following exercise. (See Figure 9-14.) Modulate up by half steps.

Objective No. 2: Singing soft with intensity. Simple chordal exercises and chorales are performed at forte, mezzo forte, piano, and pianissimo dynamic levels consecutively. The director ensures *increased* support for each repetition.

4. *Expression*

a. *Desirable goals.* Ensemble singers should be able to offer a wide palette of tonal colors. For example, their pianissimo should sound different when they are performing a French chanson than it does when they are singing a Russian motet.

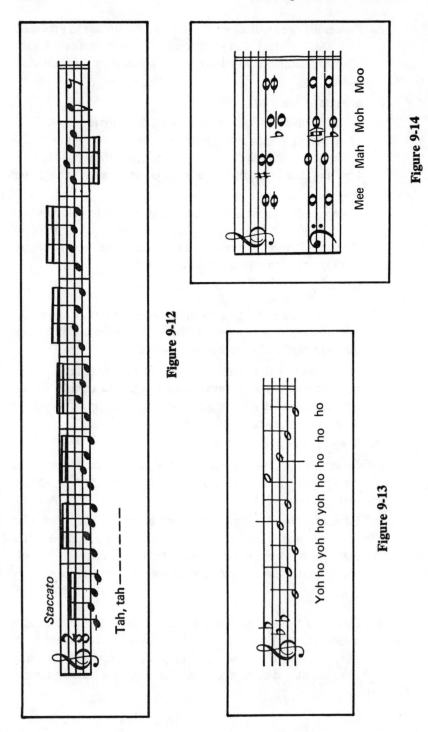

Figure 9-12

Figure 9-13

Figure 9-14

b. *Procedures*. Through the use of descriptive adjectives and imagery, the director encourages singers to perform short chordal exercises with a variety of tonal sounds. Demonstrators are helpful in correlating the desired sounds with the director's requests.

c. *Suggested exercises*

Objective No. 1: Flexibility in tonal weight. Singers perform a chordal exercise several times, changing their approach for each repetition to meet the following requests by the director:

- Sing as though you are 300-pound coal miners.
- Sing as though you are refined noblemen.
- Sing as though you are soldiers.
- Sing as though you are angels.

Objective No. 2: Emotional chordal portrayal. Singers perform exercises to the following requests.

- Make the exercise sad.
- Make the exercise happy.
- Make the exercise restful.
- Make the exercise zesty.

10

Techniques for Conducting
Effective Rehearsals

In my experiences as a choral adjudicator and consultant, I have discovered two facts:

- A vocal ensemble's success in concert can usually be predicted by the quality of its rehearsals.
- The concert performance is a reliable indicator of how effectively rehearsals have been conducted.

There is no doubt that successful choral programs are achieved through superior daily rehearsals.

REHEARSAL ACTIVITY PLANNING

Rehearsal planning is like playing chess—every move must be made with an eye on the future. Usually, the "future" means an upcoming concert. Do not, however, allow public performance to be your sole motivating factor for rehearsing. That one-hour concert, hopefully, will reward all participants with a rich experience, but what about those 40 or so hours of preparation? Consider the following goals as well when you are planning rehearsal activities:

- Enjoyment in ensemble singing
- Aesthetic experience
- Repertoire appreciation
- Choral music education

Formulating a Long-Range Rehearsal Plan

Rehearsals cannot be planned in isolation. Each must be "weighed in" as part of a series of events designed to achieve specific goals within a pre-established time schedule. Preparation for a concert can be carried out smoothly if all choral selections are prepared, *as a group,* in three different stages. To ensure adequate and proper planning, follow this step-by-step procedure.

1. Refer to your Planning Calendar for the next concert date (see Chapter 4 for a discussion of planning calendars and how to compute rehearsal time).

2. Prepare a separate *Rehearsal Plan Calendar* (see Figure 10-1) by blocking in the following phases:

- Phase I—Note Learning and Technical Mastery
- Phase II—Polishing
- Phase III—Interpreting

These three phases were briefly mentioned in Chapter 4 as a logical way to prepare an entire concert program with perspective and thoroughness.

3. Consider which types of rehearsals will best accomplish your objectives within each of the three phases. Select them from the following list and note where you plan to use them on your Rehearsal Plan Calendar:

- Sectional
- Regular
- Solo
- Instrumental
- Combined
- Dress

The Daily Rehearsal Plan

Similar in purpose and format to the lesson plan used in classroom teaching, the Daily Rehearsal Plan serves as a guide for structuring an individual rehearsal. (See Figure 10-2.) Note that space is provided for "Supplemental Activities." These could include developmental en-

REHEARSAL PLAN CALENDAR

SUNDAY	MONDAY	TUESDAY	WEDNESDAY	THURSDAY	FRIDAY	SATURDAY
SEPTEMBER S M T W T F S 5 6 7 8 9 10 11 12 13 14 15 16 17 18 19 20 21 22 23 24 25 26 27 28 29 30	NOVEMBER S M T W T F S 1 2 3 4 5 6 7 8 9 10 11 12 13 14 15 16 17 18 19 20 21 22 23 24 25 26 27 28 29 30				1	2
3	4 11 A.M. Regular PHASE I →	5 11 A.M. Sectional: "Work X"	6 11 A.M. Regular	7 11 A.M. Sectional: "Work Y"	8 11 A.M. Regular	9
10	Columbus Day 11 11 A.M. Sectional: "Work Z"	12 11 A.M. Regular PHASE II →	13	14	15 ↑	16
17	18 No rehearsal (Convocation)	19 11 A.M. Regular 4 P.M. Solo	20 11 A.M. Regular with Soloists PHASE III ↑	21 1 P.M. Instrumental	22 ↑ ↑	23
Yom Kippur 24	Veterans Day 25 11 A.M. Combined On Stage →	26	27 4 P.M. Technical	28 4 P.M. Dress	29 8 P.M. CONCERT ↑	30
Halloween 31						October

Figure 10-1

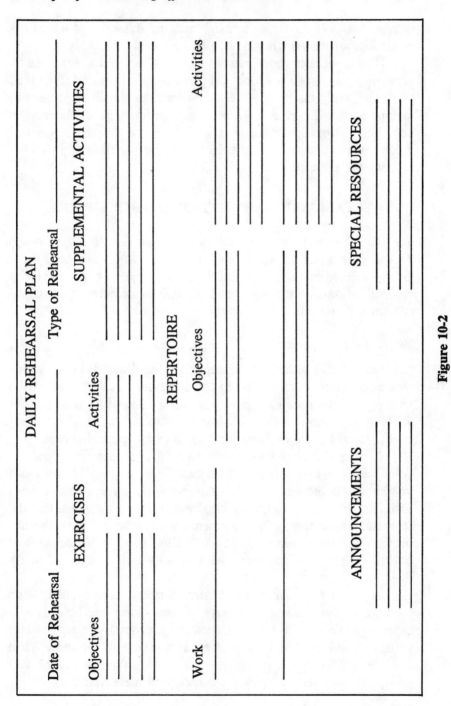

Figure 10-2

deavors such as ear training and sight reading. Listening to recordings or electing officers might also be listed under this category.

During visits to choral rehearsals, I have noticed a reluctance by some directors to use any kind of a plan. When questioned about this, they often reply that they prefer to take a more creative approach to making music. Unfortunately, these same directors quite often end up complaining about insufficient rehearsal time, and their singers will voice concern that the ensemble lacks purpose. Remember, creativity without any sense of direction is chaos.

ESTABLISHING OPERATIONAL PROCEDURES

The rehearsal may be well planned, but its effectiveness will depend on the way in which activities are presented and conducted. Overly methodical rehearsals fail to generate a feeling of spontaneity and enthusiasm. On the other hand, guidelines are necessary to facilitate smooth and efficient operation.

Rehearsal Principles

Successful leaders learn to recognize "fundamental laws" within their profession which can be violated only at risk. What would be your reaction to a football coach who never allowed his team to punt the ball on fourth down? Rehearsals are also subject to several principles. Do not overlook them for other than exceptional reasons.

1. *Begin and end the rehearsal with high-interest repertoire.* After the initial exercises have been completed, move right into music you know will produce an enthusiastic response. Save announcements until later when the singers will also benefit from a short rest. End the rehearsal by performing for enjoyment a work which the ensemble has been meticulously preparing. This will allow them to appreciate their efforts. Or choose a previously learned work which they particularly like.

2. *Plan for variety in activities.* Singers become bored when they are required to work too long on one choral selection. This is especially true when conductors attempt to accomplish note-learning, polishing, and interpreting of a single composition all at once. When you are rehearsing a major-length work, move through several sections, perhaps even out of normal order, to achieve variety.

3. *Keep singers invigorated.* Did you know that the imminence of bad weather (falling barometric pressure) causes poor singing? High humidity also has a detrimental effect on intonation. But, despite these problems, or even complacent ensemble response, the show must go on. Here are four ways to invigorate your singers.

- Keep the group on its toes by surprising them with unexpected changes in tempo, delayed cues, key changes, and so on.
- Tell a joke, or capitalize on humorous situations which develop in rehearsal.
- Alternate between group sitting and standing. Get people moving, even while they are singing.
- Plan for breaks or short intermissions when you are rehearsing for more than one hour.

4. *Establish a realistic pace.* Let's face it, some days are "off days" for your ensemble. In other instances you may have set standards which are unrealistic for a new choral situation. If, in spite of your efforts, you cannot reach planned objectives, be prepared to settle for what you can get. As a rule, try to set and maintain a realistic pace by keeping no more or less than one step ahead of your performers at all times.

5. *Make efficient use of time.* Any instance in which a singer is not engaged in some form of musical activity is a waste of time. Do not expect a vocal section to sit and watch you rehearse others for more than five minutes. Plan sectional rehearsals or stagger the arrival and departure of individual sections if you must rehearse a section for more than five minutes. Good choral rehearsals can be characterized as musically purposeful; poor rehearsals are disruptive.

Mechanics of Operation

All organizations adopt procedures so that they may function as smoothly as possible on an everyday basis. Experience has shown that certain mechanics of operation are necessary for an efficient choral rehearsal.

1. *Get each choral member into the habit of using a pencil.* Singers are usually very optimistic about their ability to remember all of the information you provide about changes in the music. Slowed

rehearsals and occasional memory lapses in performance have proven otherwise.

2. *Give musical locations with precision:* "Begin on page seven, the fourth brace, the second measure, the third beat." Repeat the location and then promptly begin. When you are referring to locations strictly by rehearsal letters or numbers, try to resume at these designators. If you must begin at a place in between, use the following format: "From rehearsal letter (or number)_____ count forward (or backward) with me." Then proceed to count out loud as you move toward the spot at which you plan to begin.

3. *Establish a standard procedure for handling divisi choral scoring.* Designate individual singers to perform specific parts whenever the scoring expands from its normal pattern.

4. *Coordinate rehearsal plans with accompanists.* As a minimal courtesy, they should be told in advance which choral selections you plan to rehearse so that they may practice. Other useful information would include the following:

- Initial rehearsal and final concert tempos
- Difficult choral phrases requiring demonstration by the accompanist
- How you intend to conduct passages requiring close musical coordination

If new exercises are to be introduced, show the accompanist how you intend to execute them.

Seating Arrangements

Many choral directors fall into the habit of using the same standard seating arrangement for all rehearsals and concerts, regardless of changes in circumstances which might dictate a better solution. As a matter of fact, some important studies have been undertaken in an attempt to determine the effects of various arrangements on both performers and audiences. Here are some useful facts:

1. The conventional arrangement of placing voices in sections works best for learning music, especially by nonselect singers. Individuals out of tune, however, may tend to pull an entire section off pitch. Audiences prefer this format when they are listening to contrapuntal music; they can hear the semi-independent performance of each section in stereophonic relief.

2.   Singers placed in mixed quartets tend to develop self-reliance and a stronger sense for the contextual relationship between their vocal part and others. Problems in blend and balance may occur whenever individuals from one voice part are required to sing passages together. Audiences like the mixed-quartet arrangement for homophonic (chordal) performance because they hear a more cohesive choral sound.

From my personal experience I have found that the mixed-quartet format works well with chamber-sized ensembles where overall group blend becomes a premium consideration. These smaller groups also seem to develop empathy more readily when they are intermixed. For larger ensembles, however, I prefer sectional arrangements. This way I can control balances, mold individual lines, and give specific cues.

One obvious way to benefit by both formats during rehearsals is to use what I refer to as an "alternating seating plan."

- For Phase I activities (Note Learning and Technical Mastery) use the sectional plan to secure pitches and build initial confidence in performing new music.

- For Phase II (Polishing) switch to the mixed-quartet arrangement to develop musical interplay between singers. I also like to use other formats such as a circle or circles within circles to increase empathy.

- For Phase III (Interpreting) return to the original plan to refine sectional contributions.

In my opinion, the most important issue in this discussion about seating is not the advantages of the sectional versus the quartet plan, but which configuration you will choose within the sectional format. For example, where should a weak tenor section be placed in relation to the other parts? Obviously, factors such as appearance, available space, lines of sight, and compositional scoring will affect your choices. Here are some typical solutions for unusual situations.

1.   Weak men's sections

Note: Placing extreme
ranges behind each
other improves
tuning and blending.

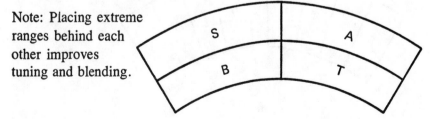

2. Fewer men than women

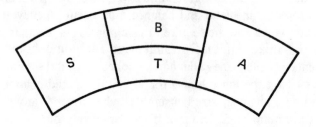

3. SATB to SS^{2}ATT^{2}B within a work or program

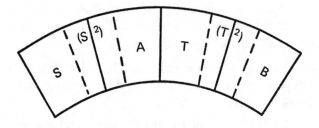

4. Use of an echo choir on stage

5. Antiphonal arrangement between two similar-sized choirs

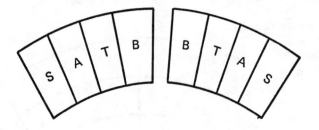

6. Projection of theme in cantus firmus types of compositions

Regardless of which seating arrangement you choose, there are several points to consider.

1. Allow for adequate spacing between singers. Remember, a cramped ensemble produces a *smaller* sound.
2. Place contrasting voices next to each other. This placement can be determined by vocal strength, musical experience, sight reading ability, musicianship, and vocal limitations. Avoid placing strident voices together, or you will compound their harshness.
3. Whenever possible, choose a semi-circle formation over a straight line. Your performers will hear themselves better.
4. Establish final standing arrangements well before the concert. Singers need to adjust to their neighbors.

CHORAL DICTION

Diction, as related to singing, is so important that entire books have been written on the subject. If there is one ingredient which tends to "separate the sheep from the goats" in terms of choral expressiveness, it is diction. According to Van A. Christy, "Proper attention to this one element alone can make a surprisingly good chorus from mediocre talent."[1] The purpose of this discussion is to emphasize those factors which contribute to good diction and to suggest some directions to take when you are attempting to improve your ensemble's treatment of the text.

---

[1]Van A. Christy, *Glee Club and Chorus* (New York: Schirmer Books, A Division of Macmillan Publishing Co., Inc., 1940), p. 44.

The Necessity for Specialized Study

Choral directors need to study basic principles of diction and should have the ability to at least pronounce commonly used languages accurately. While attending The Juilliard School, I was required to study English, Italian, German, and French diction for one year each. Yet, in spite of this concentrated effort, I know that I still need further study or possibly a refresher course. In order to effectively aid your ensemble with diction and textual interpretation, you should become proficient in the following areas:

1. Knowledge of the International Phonetic Alphabet (IPA), including its symbols
2. Ability to pronounce IPA sounds accurately
3. Mechanistic knowledge of how to shape the mouth, position the tongue, and so on in order to pronounce various vowels, consonants, and diphthongs
4. Ability to pronounce all words accurately in choral works selected for performance
5. Knowledge of natural stresses and elisions (slurring) inherent in each language
6. Ability to translate foreign texts. This also requires a basic knowledge of sentence structure. See Chapter 3 for a list of diction books.

The Reasons for Good Choral Diction

Knowing why proper diction is important will help you to channel your efforts when you are working with ensemble singers. Good diction is necessary for the following reasons:

1. *To improve tone quality.* Vowels are the vehicles of tone quality, and any improvement in them will have a beneficial effect on the choir's vocal sound. Properly enunciated consonants help to focus vowels.

2. *To give coherence to the text.* Listeners who understand the language your ensemble is performing should be able to *comprehend* the textual content of each choral work.

3.   *To avoid regional dialects.* Choral repertoire is international in scope and does not benefit by the addition of such ingredients as Bronx accents or Texas drawls.

4.   *To give performances a more polished effect.* The audience may not understand your foreign languages, but they will know the difference between sloppy and precise articulation of words.

Improving Pronunciation during Phase I of Rehearsals

The presentation of a choral work using superior diction is a goal best achieved through specific steps taken at each of the three phases necessary to prepare music for performance. During Phase I (Note Learning and Technical Mastery), accurate *pronunciation* of the text should be your primary concern. Five types of errors frequently occur.

1.   *Use of the wrong vowel.* For example, singers forget to change their pronunciation of the definite article "the" when it precedes a vowel. Failure to differentiate between the open and closed version of the same vowel is another problem. For instance, "è" is pronounced open, whereas "e" is spoken closed in Italian.

2.   *Careless substitution of one consonant for another.* In an effort to bring out the final consonant in the word "eyes," your performers may fall into the trap of singing "ice." This is just one example of consonants pronounced differently from their appearance in spelling. How should the German word "ewig" be sung?

3.   *Improper treatment of diphthongs.* Singers residing in the southern part of our country sometimes have a tendency to avoid the second (vanishing) vowel in diphthongs. The word "thy" becomes "thah." On the other hand, vocalists performing in a popular style often exaggerate the vanishing vowel, and such words as "try" become "trah*eeee.*"

4.   *Avoidance of the neutral vowel.* Also known as the "schwa," the "uh" sound holds an important place in English, French, and German pronunciation. Please keep in mind that the neutral vowel is necessary to give coherence to texts and can be sustained in singing like other vowels. All four "e" vowels in the French excerpt ". . . comme ce cygne qui nage . . .," taken from

Hindemith's chanson *En Hiver,* should be performed as neutral vowels.

5. *Mispronunciation of prefixes.* When ending in "e," prefixes are often pronounced as "ee." This is correct for such words as "defrost," but avoid remarks like "I am deelighted." Use "ih" instead of "ee" when appropriate.

Developing Enunciation during Phase II

During Phase II (Polishing), you should emphasize *enunciation* of the text. This refers to the clarity with which words are pronounced or, put in choral language, getting the words accross to the audience. Some typical problems are listed.

1. *Sloppy enunciation of initial and final consonants.* Watch especially for "d," "t," "h," "k," and "p."

2. *Too much emphasis of the American "r,"* resulting in a gargled sound and lack of authenticity in the case of foreign languages. Show singers how to flip and roll the "r" where necessary.

3. *Tendency to lose clarity of diction when performing softly.* Although vowels can carry well in pianissimo singing, consonants need forte treatment at all times.

During Phase II it is also important to stress *coordination* of ensemble diction.

1. Insist on uniform attacks and releases of initial and final sibilants ("s," "z," and so on).

2. When final "d," "b," and hard "g" precede a consonant or pause, make sure that the extra but necessary "uh" sound is enunciated clearly.

3. Facilitate elision between syllables and words by getting singers into the habit of attaching consonants to the *next* vowel whenever appropriate.

Cultivating Expression during Phase III

At this point, your ensemble should be in a position to emphasize *expression* of the text. When you bring out the textual meaning within the choral score, the interpretive and expressive qualities of the music itself will begin to emerge. This is primarily achieved through emphasis of important words and stress of key syllables. Regardless of language, look for the following textual clues:

1. Verbs expressing strong feeling or action (love, fight)
2. Descriptive adjectives (beautiful, stormy)
3. Subjects and objects

Coloristic effects may also be obtained during Phase III by "leaning" on certain consonants.

1. Final "m" or "n" in a musical phrase may be prolonged.
2. Initial consonants may be held slightly longer for dramatic impact (great, weep).

PREPARING CHORAL MUSIC—PHASE I

As was initially pointed out, the preparation of a choral work should be viewed as a three-phase process for purposes of planning and reaching goals. This, of course, does not imply that you should come to a screeching halt in the middle of a rehearsal because a certain phase has just been completed, nor does it mean that all selections should reach the same goal at exactly the same time. The transition into a new phase should be fluid and natural, with considerable overlapping caused by differences in the demands of each choral work.

Phase I is primarily devoted to note learning and technical mastery of the music. According to Leonhard and House, in their highly regarded book *Foundations and Principles of Music Education,* "The process of teaching music has been analyzed as a three-phase pattern of (1) synthesis, (2) analysis, (3) synthesis."[2] This approach has proven to be particularly suitable for teaching choral repertoire. Your task is to guide the ensemble through each step, using teaching strategies and learning aids necessary to best accomplish the job.

Synthesis (A)

Choral directors sometimes make the mistake of picking apart a

---

[2]Charles Leonhard and Robert W. House, *Foundations and Principles of Music Education* (2nd ed.; New York: McGraw-Hill Book Company, 1972), p. 287.

work right from the beginning. The trouble with this approach is that performers never gain an overview or perspective until after the music has been learned. Insight saves time!

Begin by providing any background information you can offer about the selection. This may mean translating part of a foreign text, defining the genre of the work, or even informing your choir about the original purpose of the composition. Besides helping to "sell" the work, this initial orientation can be important in establishing the group's attitude toward the score.

Now, the ensemble is ready to make its first acquaintance with the actual music. Somehow the singers need to become initially familiar with the entire composition. This is usually accomplished through sight reading, but there are other effective methods.

1. *Scanning.* Rather than reading each and every note, the choral group looks through the score as the director points out form, contrasts in compositional technique, unifying or recurring material, and so on. Portions of the score should be sung in the initial perusal. This approach is especially suitable for large, multi-sectional works.

2. *Demonstration.* Another obvious method is to play a recording of the music, if available. For extended-length works this may necessitate playing individual sections during several rehearsals. Sometimes a core of good sight readers or singers who have previously performed the selection can be utilized for demonstration.

3. *Singing with a recording.* Some purists might look down on this method. There are instances, however, where singing along with a record or tape recording will save valuable rehearsal time. One interesting innovation is the use of a quadrophonic tape system. Each individual line in four-part music can be prerecorded, either by keyboard or singer, on one of four tracks. Vocal sections then group themselves in front of the appropriate loudspeaker and are able to hear and perform their part contextually. This approach is very useful for learning difficult contemporary music.

Analysis

At this point, the singer is ready to become absorbed in a detailed study of the music. The conscientious conductor has already prepared his score and noted likely places of difficulty. Now he is ready to solve note-learning problems through a process of what I call "compartmentalization.'' Simply put, this means isolating problems and removing as many extraneous factors as possible. For example, if singers are having rhythmic difficulties, slowing the tempo and eliminating the text will allow them to concentrate on their problem. Speaking a neutral syllable on the same pitch would simplify learning conditions even more since the factor of pitch recognition would also be eliminated. Here are some more examples of compartmentalization.

- When pitch problems occur within homophonic (chordal) music, direct singers to perform each chord slowly and without regard to exact rhythm or meter so that they may locate their pitches contextually.
- Correct rhythmic difficulties by clapping. This is especially useful when polyrhythms occur between vocal sections.

In conjunction with compartmentalization, choose teaching strategies which will help the singer correct his errors. Compartmentalization *isolates* the problem; employing proper strategies helps *solve* the problem. Those most frequently employed in learning choral music are listed.

1. *Trial and error.* Many sight-reading mistakes are corrected by repetition; more serious errors require special attention. The effective director knows how to differentiate one from the other. Solve simple problems by trial and error.

2. *Listen and sing.* Most mistakes occur because the singer does not have a mental concept of the correct solution. Often, hearing the trouble spot played or performed by a demonstrator will help. The singer should then immediately perform the music to solidify his image.

3. *Elemental commonality.* Rarely does one encounter choral music where vocal parts share absolutely no relationship with each other. Elements of commonality often include melodic themes, rhythmic patterns, and text. Considerable time and effort will be saved by rehearsing vocal sections together whenever they share similar musical content.

- When you are teaching contrapuntal music, have everyone sing subjects, countersubjects, and recurring episodic material in unison.
- Whenever problems occur because of harmonic *dissonance,*

rehearse those vocal parts together which share the most harmonic *consonance*.

4. *Superimposition*. Sometimes individual sections need to hear their music against the background of the other parts. This is best achieved by requesting the problem vocal section to perform at a relatively strong dynamic level while the volume of all other parts is suppressed.

5. *Wrong-right*. Occasionally, performers persist in singing the wrong notes in spite of repeated attention to the problem. This may be caused by an unnatural melodic line or awkward intervals. Usually, however, the difficulty results from a mental block. In these cases, instruct the vocalists to perform the music alternately wrong and right. By rejecting the incorrect version and approving the proper response, you will help them overcome their problem through reinforcement.

6. *Intervallic*. Whenever singers have difficulty with a particular interval in their music, require them to perform that interval several times in various keys. Then, return to the music and hope for improvement.

Synthesis (B)

The final stage in the music learning process can be compared to putting together a jigsaw puzzle. As each musical section becomes eligible for graduation from the analysis stage, it receives a trial run-through. A cappella performance is especially useful as a test to see if the ensemble can hold its own. Completed sections are then added together until the entire choral work has been learned.

Do not, however, always assemble sections according to their compositional order. Start with the most difficult places first since they take longer to shape up. I prefer to establish a "battle plan" which gives priority to analyzing and assembling musical sections according to their relative difficulty. This allows me to complete the work without spending an inordinate amount of rehearsal time on easier sections.

Technical Mastery

In most instances singers learn to accommodate vocal demands made by the music as they become accustomed to their part. Technical mastery, therefore, is a process which takes place at all stages of learning music. Sometimes, however, they will need your assistance in overcoming special problems. Here are some examples:

1. Unusually high notes, especially on "ih" or "ee," require covering. Ask singers to "darken" these vowels.

2. When you are confronted by lengthy fortissimo phrases, show choir members how to conserve both breath and voice by steadily grunting while singing.

Be prepared to introduce special exercises on the spot to achieve technical mastery of specific problems.

PREPARING CHORAL MUSIC—PHASE II

Once the music has been learned and placed in the voices, you are ready to begin polishing. This is a refinement process leading to the goal of accurate presentation of a composition with precise ensemble coordination. For this phase of score preparation I find a Polishing Checklist to be invaluable. While you are rehearsing the choral work, listen critically for each checklist category and take corrective action to remedy problems.

Polishing Checklist

1. Attacks and releases
   a. Standard: uniform precision in ensemble execution
   b. Corrective actions:
      - Insist on eye contact.
      - Clarify pronunciation at attack and release points.
      - Isolate and rehearse separately problematical attacks and releases.

2. Breathing
   a. Standard: total compliance with the established breathing plan
   b. Corrective actions:
      - Insist on breathing only at designated places.
      - Stress need for adequate inhalation and controlled emission of breath.

- Deliberately slow down demanding phrases to develop stamina and pacing.
- Make sure that singers do not breathe in obtrusive places when they are employing staggered breathing.

3. Intonation
   a. Standards:
      - Accurate and timely movement to pitches, especially within chords
      - Consistent preservation of pitch and key within each vocal section
   b. Corrective actions:
      - Insist on proper posture and adequate support.
      - Keep ensemble vocal production lyrical and forward in placement. Avoid chesty, throaty, singing.
      - Make sure vowels are correctly and uniformly pronounced.
      - Guard against "dipping" into successive notes on the same pitch.
      - Beware of ensemble tendency to overstep descending intervals and understep ascending intervals.
      - Avoid "key fatigue" from singing in one key too long.
      - Experiment with raised and lowered keys, especially when a particular vocal section appears to have tessitura or register problems.
      - Vary accompaniment by having the keyboard played an octave higher or lower and by using staccato.
      - For accompanied choral works, switch to a cappella performance to develop ensemble pitch awareness.
      - Make sure outer vocal parts are tuned and then tune inner parts.

   Tonal intensity
   a. Standard: continual vibrancy of tone
   b. Corrective actions:

- Insist on energized consonants and rounded vowels to prevent "dead" tones.
- Stress the necessity for increased support when singers are singing softly.
- Ask for a "hushed" rather than a soft response.
- Strive for controlled, resonant singing of loud passages. Do not permit shouting or blatancy.

5. Rhythm and tempo
   a. Standards:
      - Precise execution of note values
      - Accurate initiation and maintenance of conductor's tempo
   b. Corrective actions:
      - Do not accept rhythmic discrepancies between individual singers.
      - To define exact moment of entry for each note, request choir to perform music staccato.
      - Practice the opening measure of the composition at various speeds to establish ensemble compliance.
      - When you encounter difficulty in maintaining a steady tempo, ask the singers to pulsate their music by accenting each pulse beat while singing.

6. Dynamics
   a. Standards:
      - Observance of all dynamic markings
      - Clarity of contrast between dynamic levels
      - Smooth control of crescendos and decrescendos
   b. Corrective actions:
      - Clarify which dynamic levels are required and then move to each marking and rehearse for accuracy in volume.
      - Verbally warn singers of upcoming dynamic markings as they perform the music.
      - Specify exactly where crescendos and decrescendos

begin and end. For extended ones, ask singers to write in dynamic levels as sign posts above designated notes.

7. Articulation
   a. Standards:
      - Observance of all articulation markings
      - Clarity of contrast between required articulations
   b. Corrective actions:
      - Demonstrate required articulations. Show the difference between accents and stresses, staccato and marcato, and so on.
      - Verbally warn singers of upcoming articulations as they perform the music.

8. Blend
   a. Standard: uniformity of ensemble sound; no voices stick out
   b. Corrective actions:
      - Insist on a smooth, composite sound, especially when vocal sections have "solos."
      - Avoid edgy or "pinched" tone quality. Request singers to incorporate a "yawn" feeling into their singing.
      - Work with sections down to quartets or even to duets to achieve uniformity of sound.
      - Tactfully modify individual response if it destroys ensemble blend.

9. Balance
   a. Standards:
      - General equalization of tonal weight between vocal sections
      - Sectional sensitivity to dynamic give-and-take when required in the music
   b. Corrective actions:
      - To achieve equal weight, require all sections to match volume with that produced by the *weakest* vocal part.
      - Specify places where musical material should be brought out or subordinated by individual sections.

- To promote awareness of give-and-take in rehearsal, instruct performers to sing words only when they are presenting thematic material. Otherwise, when presenting subsidiary material, they should hum or sing a specified vowel.

PREPARING CHORAL MUSIC—PHASE III

Have you ever ordered the specialty of the house at a gourmet restaurant only to discover that the entree was undercooked? Such an experience can be particularly frustrating when you consider the time and energy that was necessary to prepare that delicacy—not to mention your expenditure of money. Unfortunately, choral concerts are sometimes marred by "undercooked" presentations. The true flavor of a musical work can only be brought to fruition through that final phase called interpretation.

What Is Interpretation?

This refers to the creative act of bringing out a musical work's expressive qualities. Interpretation is achieved in three ways:

- By attempting to perform the work with stylistic accuracy (fully covered in Chapter 7)
- By observing the expressive features contained within the choral composition
- By carefully adding subjective nuances to further enhance the music's expressivity

Observing the Music's Expressive Features

Performing music with expressivity is synonymous with good musicianship. The difference in choral music is that the director must find ways to achieve this through his singers regardless of their present musical status. Locating expressive features is best achieved in conjunction with score analysis (see Chapter 8).

The next step is to convey these insights to your ensemble and then devise methods to bring out the expressive features. Here are some suggestions.

1. Outline the contour of important musical phrases on a chalk

board. Show where notes of tension and repose occur. Demonstrate how these points can be expressed through vocal intensity and tempo rubato. Rehearse each phrase individually until the ensemble is able to capture the proper expression.

    2.   Isolate individual chords, phrases, and sections which demand contrasting or unusual tonal expression. Demonstrate the desired effect and then rehearse performers for compliance.

    3.   Have singers underline the syllables of words which need to be stressed and then practice reading the text while incorporating these stresses.

Adding Subjective Nuance

    Regardless of how specific a composer attempts to be regarding the interpretation of his music, subjective decisions must be made by the choral director. Just how long is that fermata? How long should one pause between movements? Although there are no correct answers for these types of decisions, there is an important factor to consider called "taste." According to the *Harvard Dictionary of Music,*

> A personal interpretation is the performer's great privilege, granted him by the composer. A really fine performer is always aware of the responsibility toward the work that this privilege imposes.[3]

    Be careful not to take excessive license with the work you are interpreting. Watch especially for the following undesirable tendencies:

    1.   Cosmetic additions of expressive devices

    2.   Broadening of natural give-and-take within phrases into distinct accelerandos and rallentandos

    3   Drastic changes of tempos and dynamics

---

[3]"Interpretation," in *Harvard Dictionary of Music* (2nd ed., edited by Willi Apel, 1970), p. 418.

11

Final Preparations for Performance

Would you place an expensive painting in a cheap picture frame? Probably not, because a work of art requires a proper setting. Quality choral concerts are also works of art. Yet they are sometimes marred by improper settings caused by insufficient planning or faulty coordination. Please note that I am not referring to the performance facility. Some choral directors have access to a well-designed auditorium; others must be content to hold their concerts in a gymnasium. The setting to which I refer includes all of those factors necessary to present a choral concert smoothly and effectively.

COMPLETING ENSEMBLE PREPARATION

Memorization

There are several arguments, pro and con, concerning the performance of choral music from memory.

1. Advocates point out that singers are free to maintain continual eye contact with the director. The ensemble also makes a neater appearance without printed music, which tends to clutter the stage.
2. Those not in favor feel that the time spent memorizing the music could be better applied to improving the vocal group's ability to perform the work. Musical errors caused by memory lapses are also eliminated.

There are other factors to be considered when you are deciding whether or not the choir should memorize its music. Staging your group and planning for considerable movement or using a darkened stage to create special effects would dictate the necessity of performing without printed music. On the other hand, memorization of atonal choral works or very lengthy oratorios would be difficult and time consuming.

If you do choose to have music performed from memory, consider these helpful suggestions.

1. Begin the memorization process as an integral part of Phase II; do not wait until the last phase. As you finish polishing a musical section, ask that it be performed from memory.

2. Use an ABA approach.

   - A. Singers perform a single page or section while looking at the printed score.

   - B. They close their score and perform this material from memory.

   - A. After this, they immediately return to the printed score and perform the music a third time, making spot corrections of any mistakes or memory lapses that occurred.

3. Set a proper example by making sure that *you* have memorized the score.

4. Do not neglect previously memorized music. Periodically review those older works. This saves the time needed to rememorize an entire score.

Stamina

Performing a lengthy concert under hot lights requires strength and endurance. For unconditioned singers, a performance may begin as an artistic experience but degenerate into an uncomfortable ordeal. Then the ensemble becomes plagued by sagging pitches and loss of musical vitality. Take the following steps to build stamina:

1. Approximately two weeks before a concert, ask singers to stand for part of the rehearsal. Increase this with each rehearsal until they have become accustomed to standing for the entire rehearsal several days prior to the performance. Show them how to avoid rigidity without detracting from their concert appearance by wiggling their toes, breathing for relaxation, and so on. This will also help to prevent fainting spells.

2. Build vocal stamina by encouraging choral members to sing at concert hall volume before the date of the performance.
3. If music is to be held, make sure that folders are kept at the proper height during rehearsals to build arm strength.

Continuity

Conscientious directors are reluctant to allow improper or inferior performances to occur without stopping for correction. But I once knew a choral conductor who carried this too far; he seldom completed a concert without pausing to correct a mistake! Therefore, as the performance date is approached, the ensemble must be allowed to perform single works and then groups of compositions without interference. Only in this way will the choir members learn how to pace themselves or develop an ability to recover quickly from musical errors. Choral groups not achieving a sense of continuity run the risk of losing poise and momentum if something goes wrong.

Mental Preparation

For most choral performers, singing in a concert is an adventuresome experience requiring steady nerves. How can you prepare your singers psychologically for their concert? One obvious solution is to perform for any individuals willing to attend final rehearsals. Performing for other musicians is especially helpful since it motivates the ensemble to give their best.

Another method is to tape record the choral group; then allow the singers to evaluate their progress. Make sure, however, that you leave enough remaining rehearsal time to work out problems. When used properly, recordings can build ensemble confidence.

COORDINATION OF MUSICAL ELEMENTS

Preparation of choral selections does not, in itself, guarantee a successful concert. How will the ensemble get its pitches? What steps will be necessary to combine the contributions of vocal soloists and instrumentalists most effectively? These are factors to be considered when you are coordinating musical elements.

Preparing Soloists

Vocal solos require special attention by you. Even if a soloist is coached by a voice teacher, plan to spend time with him at least to iron out problems of musical coordination and interpretation. I find the following procedure to be effective:

1. As soon as soloists are chosen, let them know about musical decisions directly affecting their vocal part. Here are some specific examples.

    • Cuts

    • Tempos

    • Unusual changes, additions, and deletions

2. Establish a deadline for soloists to be prepared to perform their music.

3. After this deadline, try to integrate the solos into regular rehearsals. This solves many coordination problems and allows both soloists and ensemble members to become more comfortable with the music.

4. Hold a solo rehearsal to establish your interpretive concepts, work out specific tempos, and coordinate musical cues.

Combining the Choral Ensemble with Instruments

As with vocal soloists, you must plan to hold a minimum of one separate rehearsal with instrumentalists. Only in this way will you clearly hear and correct their problems. This also gives them a chance to find out how you intend to conduct the music. Then, when you hold the combined rehearsal, the instrumentalists will be in a better position to "carry the ball" if you need to devote part of your attention to the chorus.

Balance is the biggest potential problem you will face when you are working with singers and instrumentalists. Here are some remedies to consider when the instrumental ensemble covers the choir.

1. Make sure that the choral group is elevated well above the instruments so that the vocal sound will project without interference.

2. If the singing is being "swallowed" by stage curtains, use

sound deflectors or a shell. As a last resort, consider exposing the back wall of the stage.

3. Position instrumentalists so that their instruments point across stage rather than outward toward the audience.

4. Shift all instrumental dynamic markings back one level whenever possible.

Preparing the Ensemble for Another Conductor

Occasionally, you may be faced with the task of preparing a vocal group for a performance conducted by someone else. This situation occurs most frequently when the orchestra or band director in your school is chosen to conduct a combined musical work. In order for this collaboration to be fruitful for all, you must avoid the following typical problems:

- The choir is not flexible enough to comply with the conductor's interpretation.
- Choral attacks and releases are vague or muddy.
- The ensemble is not sure where to come in after lengthy interludes.
- The singers cannot find locations where the director wishes to begin.

Preparation of the ensemble for another conductor must be considered as an *extra* step to be undertaken after Phases I through III have been completed. These requirements must be satisfied.

1. *Coordinate with the other conductor.* Find out if he plans to make cuts or alter the printed score in any way. Make sure that your vocal group has the identical measure or rehearsal numbers contained in his score.

2. *Overprepare your ensemble.* Take the necessary steps to ensure yourself that the choral group can perform the work correctly in spite of insufficient cues from the podium. For example, orchestra directors do not usually pinpoint the treatment of consonants while conducting. Singers must be trained to do this independently.

If the work to be performed includes lengthy interludes, show the ensemble where to listen for musical cues occurring shortly before their entries. As a final test before turning the group over to the other conductor, see if the choir can perform its music with minimal direction.

3. *Develop flexibility.* Performing groups become so accustomed to their leader's way of doing things that they sometimes have difficulty adjusting to another conductor's interpretive ideas. You can facilitate this changeover by developing your singers' ability to perform the musical work with flexibility. During final rehearsals, change tempos, rallentandos, fermatas, and so on. Also vary your conducting style whenever possible.

Giving Pitches

Special pitches or chords necessary to begin a choral work should be given as unobtrusively as possible during a concert. Generally speaking, it is a good idea to provide the choir with these tonal cues before the director comes on stage or during applause prior to the next selection. The mode chosen should be based on appropriateness as well as on available sources. For example, do not select a trombone when a flute is on hand. Consider the following list of potential pitch sources:

1. Pitch from within the ensemble by an individual with perfect pitch. Female voices carry the best.
2. Pitch pipe played by someone within the choral group. This mode is less obtrusive than the choral director's use of a pitch pipe.
3. Arpeggiated chord played lightly on the keyboard. I prefer the descending arpeggio because of its more buoyant effect.
4. Pitch given by a treble instrument in the orchestra

CONCERT FACILITY ARRANGEMENTS

Performance halls are usually in heavy demand. This is especially true of school auditoriums, which may be used for everything from civic functions to study halls. Make sure that you book your ensemble as early as possible for necessary rehearsals on stage as well as for the actual concert. It is also a good idea to make these requests in writing. Many a concert has been jeopardized because of confused verbal commitments.

Choosing Technical Resources

As the concert date is approaching, you should consider what available stage equipment and other physical resources will be needed to present your choral performance at its best. Use the following checklist in this planning:

- Keyboard instruments
- Risers
- Podium
- Music stands and lights
- Extension cords for lights
- Chairs
- Reflectors or concert shell
- Stage curtains and backdrop
- Lighting for the ensemble
- Special lighting for soloists
- Sound amplification

Personnel Requirements

The next step is to determine what people will be required to move equipment, operate lights, hand out programs, and so on. In some cases, several of your own choir members will need to help out as ticket sellers or, in a pinch, even as stagehands. The important thing is to determine exactly what personnel will be needed, get as much support as possible from resources outside the singing organization, and then fill in the gaps with your own people where necessary. Here is a comprehensive list of possible personnel:

- Box office ticket sellers
- Custodial staff to unlock the concert facility, to turn on house-lights, and for housekeeping
- Ticket collectors
- Ushers

- Technicians to operate lights, audio equipment, and curtains
- Stagehands to set up and move equipment
- Technicians to tune keyboard instruments

CONDUCTING THE DRESS REHEARSAL

The final rehearsal before a performance, commonly known as the "dress rehearsal," provides the director with an opportunity to mold the concert program into an artistic whole. This important rehearsal should take place at the concert facility so that proper tempos, balances, and dynamics can be determined, based on actual acoustics. Not to be overlooked are the non-musical necessities which also need to be coordinated. I prefer to divide a dress rehearsal into three stages:

- Organization of non-musical activities
- Coordination of light and sound
- Non-stop musical rehearsal

Organization of Non-Musical Activities

How will the ensemble line up and get onto stage? Where will soloists stand? These are typical problems which need to be resolved at dress rehearsal. An experienced choral group will have adopted certain procedures which do not need to be discussed or practiced at every final rehearsal. This is how I organize non-musical activities for a new choir.

1. Form the ensemble in position on stage. Check for spacing and lines of sight. Designate which individuals will lead the choral group on and off stage.
2. Warm up the performers for later performance.
3. Clarify how music will be held while singers are moving and when to open choir folders. Check to make sure that music is held at the same level by each vocalist.
4. Discuss stage deportment, if necessary. Here are some guidelines for singers.

    - Do not react or talk to individuals in the audience.

- If you are performing without music, keep arms and hands either at the side or in a specified position.
- Maintain proper posture throughout the performance.
- Look as though you are involved with the emotional content of the music.

5. Practice bowing. I ask singers to bow together at a prearranged signal, count silently to five, and then resume their attentive position. Soloists will also need guidance at this point regarding movement into position and individual acknowledgment of applause.

6. Remind singers of prescribed concert dress, arrival time before the concert, and any other necessary points of information.

7. Practice all physical movements planned for the concert. This includes the initial entrance and final exit. Stress the need to move with purpose. Do not allow individuals to zigzag up the risers.

Coordination of Light and Sound

Lighting for a choral concert may vary from simple illumination of the stage to the elaborate use of spot and colored lights. In the latter case, an extra technical rehearsal may be required to position lights properly and coordinate special effects chosen to enhance the performance. When you are making decisions regarding lighting, do not overlook one fact—the performers must be able to see you and their printed music if it is being used in the concert. First make sure that the light level chosen to illuminate the stage is adequate. Then check to ensure that any spotlights employed do not blind the singers.

One of the primary reasons for holding a dress rehearsal is to resolve possible problems of balance between performing forces. This is especially important when the final rehearsal represents the only opportunity for you to gather all performers on stage before the concert. Do not be impatient with this tedious task. It is better to be accused of being meticulous than to risk a performance tarnished by unheard soloists or a chorus inundated by its accompaniment. I utilize the following procedure when I am checking balances:

1. Rehearse musical sections performed by vocal soloists. If they are overpowered, move them as far forward as possible. If necessary, soften the accompaniment. As a last resort, consider audio amplification. Use this same approach for both instrumental and choral accompaniment.

2. Rehearse musical sections performed by individual vocal sections, female voices, and so on. Bring balances into line by modifying the volume levels of either the vocalists or their accompanying forces.

3. Rehearse the softest and then the loudest musical passages performed by the full ensemble. Make necessary adjustments.

Before plunging into the final stage of the dress rehearsal, you should determine your tempos for the works to be performed. Choose a representative passage or simply start at the beginning of each selection and experiment with several speeds until you find the ideal tempo for your acoustical conditions.

Non-Stop Musical Rehearsal

The final segment of the dress rehearsal should be devoted to a complete, uninterrupted performance of the choral program so that you and the singers can experience concert-like conditions.

I was once asked to evaluate a choral program in a rural high school. I knew the director and had high regard for his talent and abilities; yet the principal complained of mediocre concerts and low ratings in annual competitions. I visited several times and was favorably impressed by the conductor's use of rehearsal time. However, as the concert approached, I discovered two problems causing the difficulty.

1. The director treated his dress rehearsal just like any other rehearsal. Consequently, his singers were unable to bridge the gap from rehearsal to concert. Such important ingredients as purposeful movement onto stage, proper acknowledgement of bows, and so on were completely missing.

2. The director never warmed up his singers before concerts. As a result, the ensemble lacked vocal confidence and took at least two selections to "get into the swing of things." This

factor alone would seriously undermine any chances of performing well in competition.

After I explained my observations to the director and gave him
some suggestions, his concerts and competition ratings finally began to
reflect the quality of his efforts.

PRE-CONCERT ACTIVITIES

Prior to the actual concert, the ensemble should gather for warm-
up exercises and for reviewing of critical musical sections in the repertoire. Because this last-minute meeting is so important to the success of
the performance, insist that all performers arrive punctually at the
designated location.

Pre-concert activities may be held on stage. However, this often
results in a rush to get through the music before the audience arrives. It
is better to choose a spacious meeting place out of earshot from the
concert hall. Ideally, this facility should have the following accommo-
dations:

- Separate dressing areas
- Security for handbags and valuables
- Chairs for performers to relax in while waiting

The director should arrive before his singers. There are three
reasons for this:

- To make sure that things are in order for the concert. Some-
  body may have blown the organ fuse.
- To avoid getting that pushed-for-time feeling. The captain of a
  ship needs calm nerves.
- To welcome your singers when they arrive and set them at
  ease. This is especially important for young soloists.

I prefer to call a relatively early meeting time and get a good start on
pre-concert activities. This allows the performers a few minutes before
the concert to "tidy up" and "cool their heels."

Consider the following suggestions when you are planning and
conducting final pre-concert activities:

1. Before arriving, locate specific places in the music that you

wish to rehearse. Note on an index card their location and what you expect to achieve.

2. Write down on another index card important last-minute reminders you want to announce to your choir.

3. Emphasize mental alertness when you are warming up the ensemble and reviewing music.

4. "Accentuate the positive; eliminate the negative."

MINIMIZING PERFORMANCE ERRORS

It is understandable why choral directors sometimes feel as if they are at the mercy of the gods once a concert gets underway. With so many human beings involved, there is always the possibility of mishaps. Actually, there are several things we can do to control the outcome of a performance without interfering with the audience's enjoyment. Two courses of action are available:

- Develop concert sign language
- Maintain mental alertness

Develop Concert Sign Language

Several specific gestures can be worked out between you and your singers to be used when problems arise in performance. These signs should be as unobtrusive as possible. Here is a list of gestures I have found to be useful.

- Left hand finger pointed upward to raise pitch
- Finger pointed downward to control sharping
- Elevate palm upward to keep music folders at proper height
- Point at self while aligning body to improve posture
- Open and close mouth to maintain singing with dropped jaws

Maintain Mental Alertness

Most mistakes occurring in performance can be directly attributed to lack of concentration. One way to overcome this insidious problem is by reminding all to observe the following rule:

As the concert lengthens, concentrate more!

During performance, there are little things you can do to keep the ensemble members alert. If I notice an individual "going off on another wave length," I may deliberately make a face to regain the singer's alertness. Sometimes it even pays to whisper something funny between selections or to make an awkward gesture just to keep the group loose and on its toes.

Make sure that you yourself do not fall victim to inattentiveness. Be especially careful for the following:

- Critical cues
- Surprise changes in meter
- Sudden dynamics at page turns
- Important tempo changes

Always strive to stay on top of every concert situation. For example, by thinking ahead, you will remember to acknowledge soloists and accompanists for audience applause.

Index

A

Accompanists, 68, 97, 180, 206
Accountability, 83-87
Acoustics, 79, 101, 204-206
Aesthetic content in choral
    music, 95-96
Agility in singing, 169-170
Alto voice, 152
Articulation, 19, 194
Attacks and releases, 166-167, 191
Attendance, 45, 85
Audiences, 100-101, 108-109, 185
Auditions:
    constructing test, 73-74
    organizing, 70-73
    publicizing, 69-70
Avenues of director growth, 57

B

Balance, 168, 194, 205-206
Baritone voice, 153
Baroque Era:
    general characteristics, 120-121

Baroque Era: *(cont.)*
    improvisation, 123
    instrumental considerations, 124
    performers, 121-122
    stylistic requirements, 122
Bass voice, 153
Baton, 35-37
Blend, 111, 167-168, 194
Body language, 30-34
Bowing by singers, 205
Breathing, 161-165, 191-192
Budget, 83-85

C

Calendars for planning, 76, 175-176
Character Analysis, 139-142
Chironomy, 115-116
Choral director roles:
    as catalyst, 49-50
    as diversified communicator, 15-18
    as leader, 38, 42, 47
    as learner, 63-64
    as monitor of proper singing,
      149-150

Choral director roles: *(cont.)*
    as performer, 64
    as viewed by choral group, 42, 44
    as vocal technician, 147
Choral groups:
    administration, 83-87
    behavior patterns, 41-42
    flexibility, 21
    general purpose, 66-67
    group dynamics, 49-52
    guidelines and rules, 44-45
    matching repertoire with, 98-99
    musical purpose, 43-44
    preliminary estimates, 67-68
    seating, 180-183
Choral history, 56
Choral periodicals, 60
Church planning, 76
Classic Period:
    general characteristics, 124-125
    improvisation, 126
    performers, 125
    stylistic requirements, 125-126
Cohesion in choral groups, 50-52
Cold, common, 156
Communication, 15-18, 135, 208
Compartmentalization in learning,
        188-190
Compatible conducting, 21-28
Concert facilities, 101-102, 202-204,
        207
Concerts:
    choosing technical resources, 203
    employing sign language during,
        208
    lighting, 205
    locating potential concerts, 74-75
    personnel requirements, 203-204
    planning, 100-102
    programming, 102-104
    reserving concert hall, 202
Conducting:
    body language, 30-34
    cues, 19-20, 35-36
    instrumentalists, 33-37
    melding, 22-23
    passive gesturing, 24-28

Conducting: *(cont.)*
    patterns, 18-19, 21-28, 34
    shading, 29
    shaping, 29-30
    with baton, 35-37
    with empathy, 32-33
Conducting problems:
    in experimental music, 134
    in Gregorian chant, 115-116
    in sacred polyphonic music, 118
    in secular polyphonic music, 120
Continuity in performance, 199,
        206-207
Coordination:
    in raising money, 89
    of attacks and releases, 166-167,
        191-192
    of consonants, 20
    of light and sound, 205-206
    of lines of sight, 79
    of musical elements, 199-202
    of officers, 91-92
    of vocal lines, 145
    through gesticulation, 15-16
    with accompanists, 180
    with other organizations, 68, 75
Corrective exercises, 164-168
Cues, 19-20, 35-36
Cyclic process in singing, 147-150

D

Daily rehearsal plan, 175-178
Demonstration, 17, 149, 188
Deportment, 204-205
Developmental exercises, 168-173
Diction:
    director skills, 55, 184
    enunciation, 186
    expression, 186-187
    in auditions, 73
    pronunciation, 185-186
    reasons for good diction, 184-185
Dress rehearsal, 204-207
Dynamics:
    in Baroque music, 122
    in Classic Period music, 125-126

Dynamics: *(cont.)*
  in experimental music, 133-134
  in Expressionistic music, 131
  in Gregorian chant, 115
  in Impressionistic music, 129
  in Romantic Period music, 128
  in sacred polyphonic music, 117
  in secular polyphonic music, 119
  standards and corrective actions,
    193-194
  to develop support, 163
  to improve balance, 168

E

Education, 90, 97, 100, 174
Empathy, 32-33, 181
Enunciation, 186
Equipment, 62-63, 81-82, 87, 101-102,
  203
Errors in performance, 208-209
Evaluation:
  by singers, 49-50, 199
  of music learning, 190
  of new music, 136
  of own capabilities, 53-56
  of rehearsal room, 78-80
  of vocal exercises, 158-159
  through auditioning, 71-74
Experimental music:
  general characteristics, 133
  interpretation, 134
  performers, 133
  stylistic requirements, 133-134
Expression, 171-172, 186-187,
  195-196
Expressionism:
  general characteristics, 130
  interpretation, 131
  performers, 130
  stylistic requirements, 130-131
Eye contact, 19, 31, 33

F

Facial expression, 30-31
Fainting, prevention, 198-199

Finances:
  estimate of available funds, 68
  maintaining budget, 83-84
  priority of financial needs, 84-85
  raising money, 87-90
Flexibility, 21, 48, 199, 201-202
Folders:
  in concert, 199, 204, 208
  repair, 87
  storage, 80-81
Foreign languages, 98, 101, 108, 139,
  184
Form and content in music, 136-138
Framing as programming device, 104
Funding, 68, 87-90

G

Gesticulation, 15-16
Golden rule of orchestral conducting,
  34
Gregorian chant:
  conducting problems, 115-116
  general characteristics, 113-114
  improvisation, 115
  performers, 114
  stylistic requirements, 114
Guidelines and rules, 44-45

H

Habitual response in conducting, 18-19
Harmonic analysis, 141
Health Checklist, 154-155
Hoarseness, 156

I

Impressionism:
  general characteristics, 128-129
  interpretation, 129
  performers, 129
  stylistic requirements, 129
Improvisation:
  in Baroque music, 123
  in Classic Period music, 126
  in Gregorian chant, 115
  in sacred polyphonic music, 118

Improvisation: *(cont.)*
    in secular polyphonic music, 120
In-between voice, 153-154
Incentives, 41-42
Instrumentalists:
    balancing, 200-201
    in early period music, 116-119,
        121-124
    working with, 33-35, 200
Instruments, 62-63, 81-82, 87,
    101-102, 203
Intensity, 171, 192-193
Interpretation:
    by adding subjective nuances,
        195-196
    by observing expressive features,
        195-196
    in experimental music, 134
    in Expressionistic music, 131
    in Impressionistic music, 129
    in Neoclassic music, 132
    in Romantic Period music, 128
    of text, 138-139
Intonation:
    affected by weather, 179
    controlling during performance, 208
    exercises, 165-166
    problems in music, 144-145
    standards and corrective actions,
        192
Invigoration, 179

K

Keyboard playing, 17, 54
Kinesics, 30-33
Knowledge necessary for directing,
    53-57, 63-64

L

Laryngitis, 157
Leadership:
    achieving personal authority, 47-49
    developing conducive environment,
        43-44
    development, 47-49

Leadership: *(cont.)*
    encouraging expressive freedom,
        150-151
    establishing guidelines and rules,
        44-45
    in choosing repertoire, 97-98
    observing leadership principles,
        45-47
    personality, 42, 47-49
    providing incentives, 41-42
    recognizing individual and group
        needs, 38-42
    remedying ensemble faults and
        weaknesses, 164-168
    solving musical problems, 142-143
    stressing vocal hygiene, 154-157
    supervising, 87, 92-94, 110
Learning, 40, 143-144, 187-191,
    195-196
Lighting, 79, 102, 205
Listening, 55, 148-149

M

Maintenance, 87
Management of choral groups, 78-94
Marking score, 145-146
Masking in body language, 30-31
Media channels in publicity, 93
Melding, 22-23
Melodic analysis, 141
Melodic perception, 162
Memorization, 162, 197-198
Mental alertness, 30-34, 162, 208-209
Mental preparation for concert, 199
Mezzo-soprano voice, 153
Morale in choral groups, 49-50
Music:
    disseminating and accounting, 85-87
    editions, 97
    publishers and distributors, 60-61
    reference copies, 60-61
    storage, 61, 80-81, 86-87
Musica ficta, 115, 118
Music before 1600, characteristics, 113

N

Neoclassicism:
  general characteristics, 132
  interpretation, 132
  performers, 132
  stylistic requirements, 132
Neo-Romanticism:
  general characteristics, 132
  performers, 132-133
  stylistic requirements, 133
News, types, 94
Note learning, 187-190

O

Officers:
  individual responsibilities, 91
  liason with director, 90-92
  necessity, 90-91
Operational procedures, 178-183
Orchestra conducting, 33-35
Organization:
  of auditions, 70-73
  of dress rehearsal, 204-207
Orientation for new singers, 39
Ornamentation, 112, 123, 126

P

Pacing in rehearsals, 179
Passive gesturing, 24-28
Patterns, conducting, 18-19, 21-28, 34
Performance practice, 56
Performers:
  in Baroque music, 121
  in Classic Period music, 125
  in experimental music, 133
  in Expressionistic music, 130
  in Gregorian chant, 114
  in Impressionistic music, 129
  in Neoclassic music, 132
  in Neo-Romantic music, 132-133
  in Romantic Period music, 127
  in sacred polyphonic music, 116
  in secular polyphonic music, 119
Personal authority of director, 47-49
Personality, 42, 47-49

Personal resource center, 62-63
Personnel required for concerts,
  203-204
Pharyngitis, 157
Phases, rehearsal, 77, 175, 181,
  185-196
Phrasing:
  in Baroque music, 122
  in Classic Period music, 125
  in conducting technique, 22
  in Expressionistic music, 131
  in Gregorian chant, 115
  in Impressionistic music, 129
  in Romantic period music, 127
  in sacred polyphonic music, 117
  in secular polyphonic music, 119
Physical movement, 151, 161, 179,
  198-199, 204-205
Pitches, 130-131, 202
Planning:
  auditions, 70-71
  by phases, 77
  calendar, 76, 175-176
  church, 76
  concert programs, 102-104
  concert season, 75-76
  daily rehearsals, 175-178
  general, 99-100
  long-range for rehearsals, 175-176
  pre-concert activities, 207-208
  rehearsal time, 76-77, 100
  specific, 100-102
  supplemental activities, 175-176
  vocal exercises, 159-161
Polishing Checklist, 191-195
Posture, 31, 155, 161, 208
Praise vs. criticism, 40, 43, 46
Pre-concert activities, 207-208
Preparation:
  of choral director, 57-65
  of chorus for another conductor,
    201-202
  of conductor's score, 135-146
  of instrumental ensemble, 132, 200
  of new printed music, 85-86
  of printed program, 110
  of soloists, 200

Press releases, 95
Principles of leadership, 45
Printed program:
    appeal, 108-110
    contents, 104-108
    examples, 106-107
    physical aspects, 109-110
    supervision, 110
Professional choral organizations, 60
Programming, 102-104
Pronunciation, 184-186
Publicity:
    ingredients, 93
    media channels, 93
    preparing press release, 94
    purposes, 92
    types of news, 94
Publishers' catalogues, 60-61
Punctuality, 45-46, 207
Purchasing, 84-85

R

Range, 42-47, 150, 169
Rapport, 42-47
Reading problems, 143-144
Record and tape library, 61-62
Reference books, 58-59
Rehearsal plan calendar, 76, 175-176
Rehearsal room features, 78-80
Rehearsals:
    computing rehearsal time, 76-77
    goals, 174
    mechanics of operation, 179-180
    pacing, 179
    phases, 77, 175, 181, 185-196
    planning, 174-178
    principles, 178-179
    types, 175, 176
Repertoire:
    aesthetic considerations, 95-96
    guidelines for choice, 96-97
    learning, 143-144, 187-191
    matching with choral group, 97-99
    programming for concerts, 102-104
Reward and punishment, 40
Rhythm, 142, 193

Rhythmic perception, 55, 162
Romanticism:
    general characteristics, 126-127
    interpretation, 128
    performers, 127
    stylistic requirements, 127-128
Rudimentary skills in conducting,
    18-20

S

Sacred polyphonic music:
    conducting problems, 118
    general characteristics, 116
    improvisation, 118
    performers, 116
    stylistic requirements, 116-117
    tactus, 21, 117-118
Scanning music, 188
Score analysis:
    Character Analysis, 139-142
    for form and general content,
        136-138
    for intonational problems, 144-145
    for reading problems, 143
    for technical problems, 145
    general familiarization, 136
    interpreting the text, 138-139
    theoretical insight, 56
Score locations, 180
Score marking, 145-146
Score mechanics, 56
Seating:
    arrangements, 181-183
    for rehearsal phases, 181
    sectional vs. mixed quartets,
        180-181
    spacing and placement of individu-
        als, 183
Secular polyphonic music:
    conducting problems, 120
    general characteristics, 118-119
    improvisation, 120
    performers, 119
    stylistic requirements, 119-120
Self-motivation in choral groups, 49-50

Shading and shaping in conducting, 29-30
Shielding in body language, 31
Sight reading:
    by director, 54
    in auditions, 73-74
    problems in music, 143-144
Sign language, 208
Silent score study, 55
Singers:
    attendance, 45, 85
    auditioning, 69-74
    bowing in concerts, 205
    condition, 100
    criteria for selection, 71-74
    deportment, 204-205
    desirable traits, 51-52
    health, 154-155
    individual needs, 38-40
    keeping invigorated, 179
    learning, 40, 187-191, 195-196
    potential, 68
    praise vs. criticism, 40, 43, 46
    preventing boredom, 179
    promoting mental alertness, 162, 199, 208-209
    self-motivation, 49-50
    spacing and placement, 183
    stamina, 198-199
    teamwork in performance, 150
    technical mastery of score, 190-191
    vocal ailments, 155-157
Singing:
    analytic stage, 149
    as cyclic process, 147-150
    by director, 17, 54
    expressively, 150-151, 171-172
    listening stage, 148-149
    modification stage, 149
    singing stage, 148
    with cold, 156
    with recording, 188
Skills necessary for directing, 18-20, 53-57, .63-64
Soloists:
    acknowledging in concert, 209

Soloists: *(cont.)*
    bowing and movement, 205
    crediting properly in program, 105
    embellishing Baroque music, 123
    for variety in programs, 99, 103
    motivation, 39-40
    preparation, 200
    relationship with ensemble, 150
Soprano voice, 151-152
Sore throat, 156-157
Sound analysis, 140-141
Spacing of concerts, 75-76
Stamina, 198-199
Storage facilities, 63, 80-81
Stylistic accuracy, 111-113
Stylistic requirements:
    in Baroque music, 122
    in Classic Period music, 125-126
    in experimental music, 133-134
    in Expressionistic music, 130-131
    in Gregorian chant, 114-115
    in Impressionistic music, 129
    in Neoclassic music, 132
    in Neo-Romantic music, 133
    in Romantic Period music, 127-128
    in sacred polyphonic music, 116-118
    in secular polyphonic music, 119-120
Support, 161-165, 191-192
Synthesis-analysis-synthesis in learning music, 187-190

T

Taxonomy of Choral Skills and Knowledge, 53-57
Teaching strategies, 187-190
Teamwork in ensemble performance, 150
Technical mastery of score, 190-191
Technical problems in music, 145-146
Technical resources for concerts, 203
Tempo:
    affected by acoustics, 101, 206
    avoiding drastic changes, 196
    in Baroque music, 122

Tempo: *(cont.)*
   in Classic Period music, 126
   in Expressionistic music, 131
   in Gregorian chant, 115
   in Romantic Period music, 128
   in sacred polyphonic music,
      117-118
   in secular polyphonic music, 120,
      145
   standards and corrective actions,
      193
Tenor voice, 152-153
Terminology and symbols, 56, 145
Tessitura, 73, 152-153, 192
Time beating, 21
Tonal color:
   in Baroque music, 122
   in Classic Period music, 125
   in experimental music, 133
   in Gregorian chant, 114-115
   in Impressionistic music, 129
   in Romantic Period music, 127
   in sacred polyphonic music,
      116-117
   in secular polyphonic music, 119
Tonal-oriented music, 131-133
Tonal structures, 136
Tone quality:
   adverse affects, 40, 111
   covering vowels, 167-168, 191
   evaluation in auditions, 73
   expression, 171-173
   improvement, 184, 194
   intensity, 171, 192-193
Translation of languages, 101, 108,
      139, 184
Trouble-shooting, 142-145
Twentieth century music, 130-134

V

Verbalization, 16
Vocal ailments:
   common cold, 156
   hoarseness, 156
   laryngitis, 157
   pharyngitis, 157
   sore throat, 156-157
Vocal exercises:
   corrective, 164-168
   developmental, 168-173
   evaluation, 158-159
   planning, 159-161
   warm-up, 161-164
Vocal hygiene, 154-157
Vocal problems:
   faulty singing, 21, 148, 154-155,
      194
   minimized by placement of indi-
      viduals, 183
   oversinging, 127, 162-164
   range coordination, 150
Voices:
   characteristics, 123, 151-153
   choosing repertoire, 98-100

W

Wardrobe:
   selection, 82-83
   storage and maintenance, 81, 87
Warm-up exercises, 161-164, 204,
      206-207
Workshops, conventions, and courses,
      63
Written communication, 17-18

Choral director's complete
handbook.